# More Advance Praise for *SkyMaul*

"If, like me, you've spent years searching for a Hitler-Turning-into-Werewolf nightlight, look no further. Kasper Hauser, America's best sketch absurdists, have what you're looking for."

—**Bob Fisher**, writer, *Wedding Crashers*

"It's hard to believe anything could be funnier than the *SkyMall* catalog itself, but along comes Kasper Hauser's *SkyMaul*, with dozens more hilarious (and essential!) items for your modern lifestyle."

—**Beth Lisick**, author of *Everybody into the Pool*

"So much funny! I laughed like I was 35,000 feet high and maxed out my credit cards shopping *SkyMaul*. It's the perfect gift for anyone with a brain!"

—**Cameron Tuttle**, author of *The Bad Girl's Guide to Getting What You Want*

"I enjoy *SkyMaul* so much that I'm no longer afraid of flying."

—**Matt Besser**, *The Upright Citizens Brigade*

# Praise for the Kasper Hauser Comedy Group

"Combin[ing] a hyperactive imagination with an inspired sense of lunacy, . . . this quartet is one of the few comedy teams which has rightfully earned the description 'Pythonesque.'"

> —*Time Out New York*

"They haven't unleashed themselves on the world at large yet, but San Francisco's Kasper Hauser, a four-man sketch comedy troupe, is destined for comic greatness."

> — *San Francisco Chronicle*

"I thought I knew what surreal was before I watched this quartet of Dadaist San Franciscan sketch artists. I didn't even have the first idea . . . Every single slick metropolitan sketch show . . . should be made to sit down in front of Kasper Hauser before they are ever allowed near a stage again."

> —*The Herald* (U.K.)

"Kasper Hauser treads its own unbeaten path of comic genius."

> —*Fringe Report* (U.K.)

"Much like sourdough bread, Kasper Hauser will travel far beyond the confines of San Francisco via the appealing incongruity of its mad vision."

> —*San Francisco Bay Guardian*

"... dense, dazzling comedy sketches . . . [Kasper Hauser] continually surprises with its oddly angled perspectives."

> —*The Stage* (U.K.)

# SkyMaul
The Unauthorized Catalog Parody

**Happy Crap You Can Buy from a Plane**

by

# The Kasper Hauser Comedy Group

Rob Baedeker
Dan Klein
James Reichmuth
John Reichmuth

THOMAS DUNNE BOOKS  ST. MARTIN'S GRIFFIN
NEW YORK

THOMAS DUNNE BOOKS
An imprint of St. Martin's Press

www.thomasdunnebooks.com
www.stmartins.com


Library of Congress Cataloging-in-Publication Data

Kasper Hauser Comedy Group.
        SkyMaul : happy crap you can buy from a plane / Kasper Hauser Comedy
Group (Rob Baedeker, Dan Klein, James Reichmuth, John Reichmuth)—1st ed.
                p. cm.
ISBN-13: 978-0-312-35747-4
ISBN-10: 0-312-35747-8
        1. Mail-order business—Humor. 2. Commercial catalogs—Humor. 3. Air
travel—Humor. I. Title.

PN6231.M17 K37 2006
818'.607—dc22

                                                    2006044642

10 9 8 7 6 5 4 3 2

designed by:
# Vince Bohner

contributing designers:
Charette Communication Design
Liz Craig
Arin Fishkin
Spero Nicholas
Sean Nolan
Brad Rhodes
and the Kasper Hauser Comedy Group

original photography:
Mario Parnell
Gabe Weisert

# A Message from SkyMaul's CEO . . .

**Welcome aboard, air traveler!** My name is Jerry Ponda, C.E.O. of SkyMaul, and I'm here to tell you that THIS PLANE IS GOING DOWN! Down into an ocean of fabulous product selection and unbelievable values. So put your head between your legs and start shopping!

But first, let me tell you the story of SkyMaul and how shopping saved my life.

Christmas Eve of 1988, I was in a hotel room in Las Vegas. I had been working a big account, trying to sell some kind of small machines to some guys from a different town. I had not been home in three weeks. I missed my family: my lovely wife Pfepfer, my two children, Horace and Candy, and my Labrador buddy, Melchus. I felt miserable and did not know where I had been all day. Unbeknownst to me, I'd had a gin blackout at the Pai-Gow poker table, headed back to my room, and called an escort service! When the escort, arrived, I just started bawling like a little f---ing baby. Then, an amazing thing happened: I found $8,000 in my pocket. I had been on a monster Pai-Gow run, and I didn't even know how to play that crazy game! Asian poker? Huh!?

I sobbingly offered the escort some money and told her (him? I honestly do not recall the gender of this individual) that I didn't want anything except a massage with a happy ending. She wasn't hearing any of that. She threw open the drapes, told me to get off my pity-pot, and sassed, "You're a mess. What you need is some retail therapy!"

She grabbed me and out we went. We shopped for days. We bought inflatable pool toys, scientific pillows, and remote control submarines; back massagers, pet stairs, and golf things; it did not end until the cash was gone and two cards were maxed out. But I was myself again.

When I got home, I was mobbed by my smiling family. I cried some more, went to rehab, and started this company. I knew first-hand what shopping could do. I hope it helps you as much as it did me. What a story. I'm a genius. No one but a genius could have done what I did! Ha ha ha ha ha!

> **"I'd had a gin blackout at the Pai-Gow table."**

As soon as the money started rolling in, I started hitting the Dead shows hard. Big mistake—but that's another story.

Now, more than fifteen years and thousands of great ideas later, I pledge to bring you the newest, most useful, and, indeed, the most "funtabulous" products on the planet. Treat yourself, have fun, and . . .

**Put your head between your legs and start shopping!**

*Jerry Ponda*

Jerry (The Jerr-Bear)

# THE IMAGE SHARPENER

## Reality-Canceling Headphones

Some negativity is so strong in your life that it can't even be blocked by karate, vitamins, and sleeping in. Sometimes, even pumping iron doesn't help. That's why this crazy scientist who invented some speakers in the '60s has invented one of our best products: reality-canceling headphones. Using a simple principle called "science," the professor was able to invent headphones that block all the bullshit and responsibilities in your life. You can still hear things such as the microwave going off but not babies or the doorbell or dogs.

**Bullshit**

**Responsibilities**

**Trick Questions**

**BLLBRKR. Headphones . . . $299.00**

*You need our reality-canceling headphones if . . .*

*1. Your parents and your ex- are equally stupid in terms of valuing your achievements.*

*2. Your time is being wasted and you can't work on your screenplay,* Monkey with a Robot Hand.

*3. Owning a comic book store is looking less likely.*

*4. No progress on time travel.*

# THE IMAGE SHARPENER

## iPod Shredder

Hootie and the Blowfish? Dave Matthews? "World" beats?? If your roommate's "party shuffle" is bringing you down, simply cram his iPod and his CDs into our professional iPod Shredder and rest in peace. It will also destroy his shoes, eyeglasses, and Ferrari poster.

**CDSHRED. Professional Music Shredder . . . $188.00**

Easily handles CDs, tapes, and records!

# THE IMAGE SHARPENER

## Banana-ganizer!

Bananas are the world's most popular thing, but they're hard to keep organized! Now your bananas will be stacked and ordered alphabetically, from Brazilian Dwarf to Red Cuban. Don't be late for giving a deposition or getting a haircut: grab the banana you want when you want.

**BNANARACK. Banana-ganizer . . . $89.99**

## Bandana-ganizer!

Bandanas are nothing to sneeze at when it comes to organization. Now you can keep your head scarves sorted out with our state-of-the-art bandana rack. Divide your do-rags into Pride, Gang, Biker, and Dead Head: separate but equal.

**BNDNARACK. Bandana-ganizer . . . $88.88**

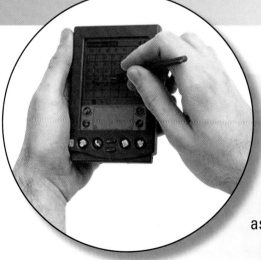

## Whore-ganizer!

Keep your sex contacts separate from your friend, family, and business numbers and sort by city. Our GPS-enabled Whore-ganizer synchronizes with your business-travel schedule to ensure that you're knee-deep in you-know-what as soon as the plane touches down.

**WHRGZR. Whore-ganizer . . . $577.00**

# THE IMAGE SHARPENER

Brainial Node

## Electric Dream Catcher

Real Indian Dream Catchers don't work! They don't catch any dreams because they don't have electricity in them. Our dream catcher has an electric web that is so tight that no dreams can get through it. Comes with a bonus electric dream pillow containing Peyote, an Indian party cactus. It's Tonto meets TiVo!

**DRMCTCHR. Dream Digital Recorder and Playback Device . . . $577.00**

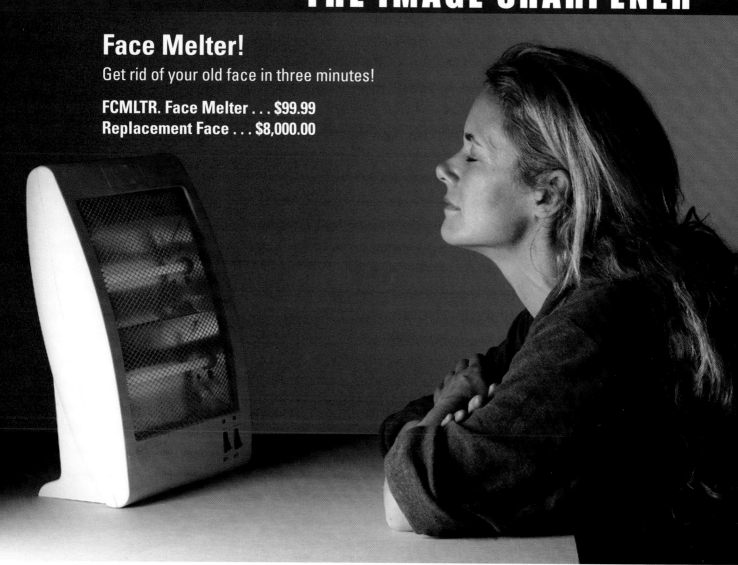

# THE IMAGE SHARPENER

## DayTripper Animal Time Machine

Send your dog on a two-minute psychedelic trip to the '70s! You won't notice a thing, but your pet will come back reeking of group sex and blonde Lebanese hash! 19 1/2"x 3 ft. (15 lbs.)

**DTRPR. Doggie Time Traveler . . . $949.00**

## Drinking Age Time Zone Watch

Where am I, beer-wise? This phenomenal watch will answer that question with the click of a button, telling you the legal drinking age anywhere in the world. If the watch says "no," just ignore it.

**BEERWCH. Drinking Watch . . . $99.00**

## Our Handcrafted Italian Sundial Simply Does Not Work

This thing looks authentic and weather-worn, but who knows what the shadow and the numbers mean? You've got VII here, and then XII over there. What? Oh, great, now it's eighteen o'clock. Totally useless, or your money back.

**SNDLCRP. Kooky Sun Dial . . . $189.00**

# THE IMAGE SHARPENER

*Blanket!*

## The Llamacycle!

The South American Indians are no dummies, especially when it comes to going up in mountains. With our new llamacycle, you get all the pack-hauling, spit-in-your-face bravado of the Andes' most reliable mini-horse combined with America's greatest invention, the Wheel!

**LLCYCL.. Llamacycle . . . $9,999.00**

*Leather pouch for llama food and bike tools.*

## HUMMER 4: Da' Earth Pig!

The newest Hummer is bigger and badder than ever. The Middle East is ours and gas prices are plummeting. With our special rear bumper adapter, your kids will be water-skiing down Main Street in a trench that you're carving out behind you. Other moms will go ape-shit!

**FCKRTH. Hummer 4 . . . $242,299.99**

Da' H4 Limited Edition Earth Pig

# THE IMAGE SHARPENER

## Japanese Thank-You Toilet

Whether it's samurai or inventing computers, the Japanese are known for what the French call savoir faire. Now bring that elegance into the toilet, with this exclusive "Thank You" potty. An electronic voice personally thanks the giver each time a load is deposited. The bigger the "gift," the louder the voice. Your kids will be fighting to go next, and what a perfect way to end a dinner party!

**DOMOAR. Japanese Thank-You Toilet . . . $888.99**
**Celebrity Voice Cartridge (please specify James Earl Jones or Reese Witherspoon) . . . $99.00**

"THANK YOU!"

## Bee Thermometer

There is only one way to know the true temperature of your bees—measure it! Our patented bee thermometer won the Apiary Science Honorable Mention in Helsinki. This thermometer can measure the temperatures of hundreds of thousands of bees, one at a time.

**BEETHRM.**
**Bee Thermometer . . . $49.99**

## Bird Zapper!

It's the law: did you know that you *own* the air over your house and yard? Don't let these entitled "feathered friends" fly into your zone. One touch, goodbye.

**BRSPR. Bird Zapper . . . $119.00**
**Broom . . . $5.00**

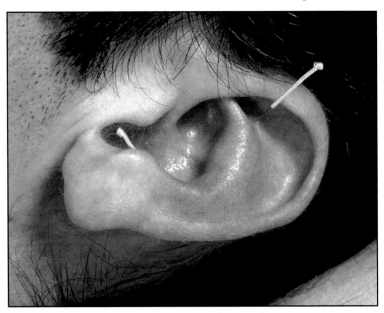
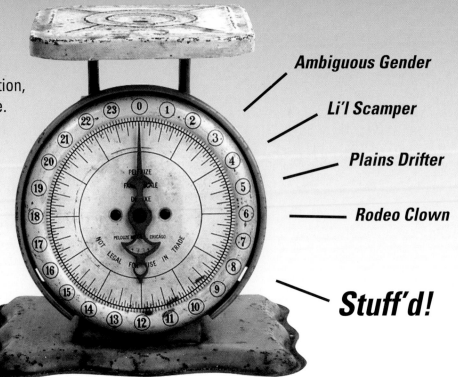

# Shop till you drop . . . from the sky!

## THE IMAGE SHARPENER

### Hitler-Turning-into-Werewolf Nightlight

This teeth-chattering hallucinosphere will light up any baby's life. Halfway between Hitler and Werewolf, it's hard to tell if it's coming or going!

Our new "monitor" function allows the wolf's eyes to follow you or your baby around the room and emits a "safety growl" anytime someone moves toward it.

**HITWLF. Wolf Hitler Light . . . $99.99**
*Wrong. Don't Do It.*

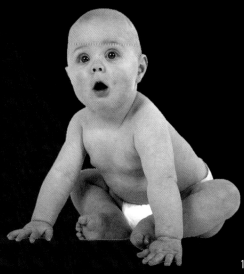

19

# THE IMAGE SHARPENER

## Divorced Dad "Pancake Time" Trumpet

Don't let those lazy teenagers sleep in
on a weekend :-)

Saturdays are legally your days: you've
made your famous blueberry pancakes,
and this goofy horn is just the kind of
wacky kind of thing you're known for.

Tell them to rise and shine by blowing some
bullshit on this Austrian parade trumpet.

They'll thank you for it . . . later!

**DVRTRM. Pancake Trumpet . . . $59.99**

## His and Hers Fire Extinguishers

Each tank and hose combo is lovingly
cloisonned in gender colors: playful
pink-red for her, masculine beef-rojo
for him. You can spray them at each
other after having sex, or use them on
a fire!

**FRCPL. His/Hers Extinguishers . . . $88.00**

*"It was fun and safe to spray each
other down."*
—Darryn Steegan

# THE IMAGE SHARPENER

## The "Cut Above"

### Electronic Hair-Salon-Naming Computer

Without a good name, your hair-salon business and your family might "dye"! That's why we have produced a "pun"-believable electronic encyclopedia of 100,000 "perm"-fect names for your new hair salon. You will feel "sheer" delight at this compre-"hair"-sive list of great salon, barbershop, and hairstylist shop names! Every new salon owner's first big test is picking a great name for their business. Don't "blow" it.

The database offers classic names:
- The Hairport
- Hair Today, Gone Tomorrow
- From Hair to Eternity

And unique and creative new salon names:
- Hair Baby, Hair's Some Money
- Hair-y Potter
- Shave Me, I'm Drowning

As well as new-school names:
- Split-Endz
- A Little Off the Sidez
- Sheer D-Lightz
- Hairly Legal

It also includes old favorites:
- Banged 'n' Feathered
- Hairy Dean Stanton
- Hair Apparent
- The Trim Job

and many, many, more ...

A must have for the new salon owner, with more "bangs" for the buck. Add additional modules to help you name your scone cart ("Scone Fishing"!), coffee shop ("Burial Grounds"!), or crepe restaurant ("The Date Crepe"!).

**HARPNZ. Electronic Hair-Salon-Naming Thing ... $199.99**

*Gettin' down to business at "Banged 'n' Feathered"*

# THE IMAGE SHARPENER

## Air Straightener

### *Stop Breathing Disorganized Air!™*

It has been more than 150 years since an English botanist noticed that particles follow a random path, making zigzags and unpredictable movements, bouncing off of different kinds of shit, including *actual* shit. This includes the air molecules that you breathe!

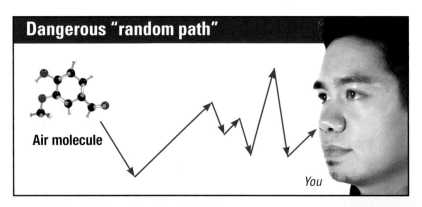

**Dangerous "random path"**

Air molecule

*You*

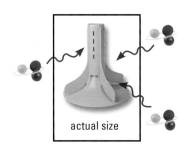

actual size

Every human being has two air bags in their chest called "lungs." These miraculous organs do everything from storing mucus to letting us smoke joints to helping us blow things. Don't let these "nature's natural miracles" get filled up with dog shit and ruin your birthday!

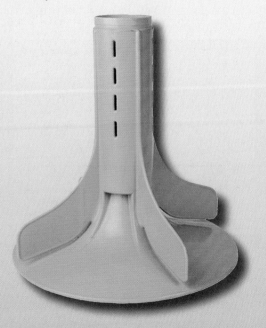

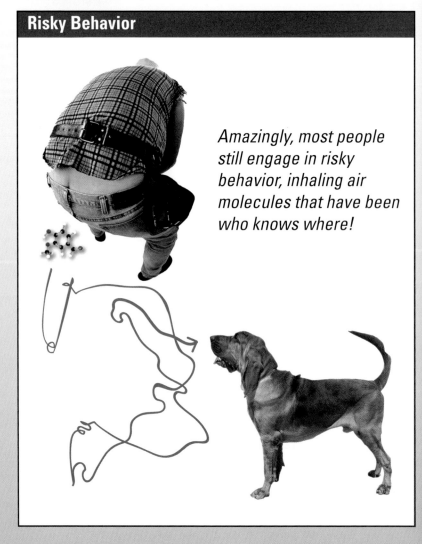

**Risky Behavior**

*Amazingly, most people still engage in risky behavior, inhaling air molecules that have been who knows where!*

# Shop till you drop . . . from the sky!

# THE IMAGE SHARPENER

## How It Works . . .

**1.** Four Entry Portals™ begin the straightening process.

**2.** A "Vacuum Tube" uses complicated science formulas to get the molecules on track.

$$f = -x^{(2) - ab}$$

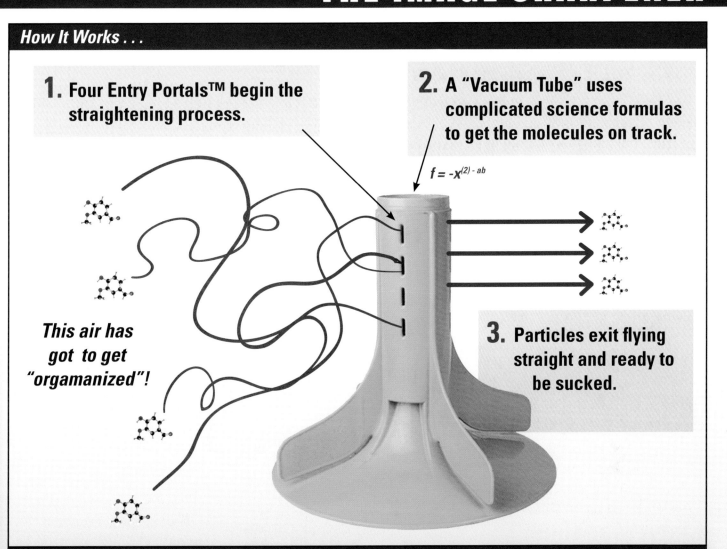

*This air has got to get "orgamanized"!*

**3.** Particles exit flying straight and ready to be sucked.

---

## Turbo "Winds of Change" Next Generation Professional Series IV

You wouldn't trust an army where the soldiers were running around all different ways. Why have that same thing going on up in the air that you're breathing!?

**AIRSTR. Air Straightener . . . $199.99**

---

### Free Gift Worth $59.99

This "Mini Winds of Change" filter will straighten out particles in your tent, RV, or bunker. Yours FREE if you give us your credit card and Social Security numbers!

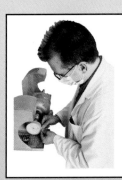

*Actual, unretouched photo of a scientist doing some work with a molecule.*

23

# THE IMAGE SHARPENER

## Stroller Mower

Don't let family get in the way of yardwork! Our combo stroller/mower is 24hp and cozy. Strap the kid in and mow down any lawn, yard, or field. Your spouse and your neighbors will thank you, and you will soon be known as a loving parent who does not spend all of his Saturdays playing online poker.

**DANGER. Baby Mower . . . $389.99**

## Sixty-Year Timer
### *Set it and forget it!*

Need a reminder to graduate? Get married? Have a mid-life crisis? Don't miss out on life's big stuff: set an alarm! Our sixty-year timer has easy-to-read settings and will emit a normal-sounding "ding" to keep you on track.

**60YRTMR. Life Timer . . . $59.99**

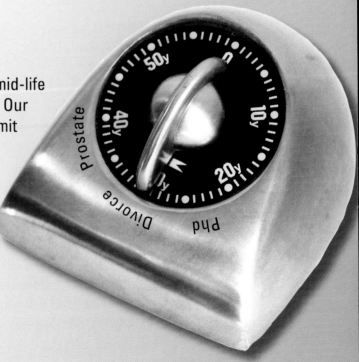

*"Ding!"*
*Time to retire.*

# Happy crap you can buy from a plane!

## THE IMAGE SHARPENER

## The First-Ever Milk Vacuum!

Is someone making assumptions about how you like your breakfast? Not a problem: our patented Lac-uum™ will suck out the milk quick, returning your cereal to its dry state, the way nature intended.

**MLKVCM. Lac-uum™ Milk Vac . . . $89.99**

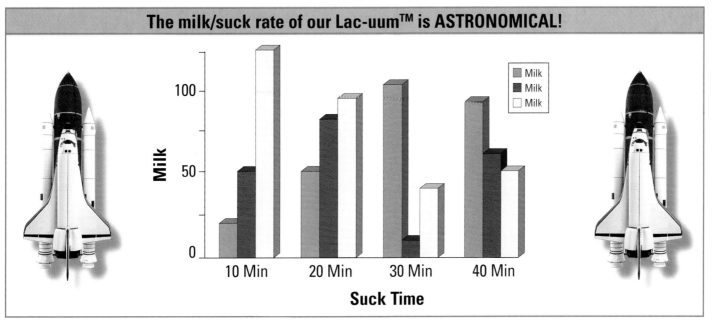

The milk/suck rate of our Lac-uum™ is ASTRONOMICAL!

# THE IMAGE SHARPENER

## R2-D3, The Homeless Robot

Hung out with C-4PO in the alternate universe *Star Wars*. It's his own fault he's like this: there are plenty of jobs for droids.

Painstakingly junked together in crap.

**BLSTRBT. Classic Shit Robot . . . $2,958.90**

## Masturbation "Whodunit?" Kit

This home crime lab will let your family's HarDee Boys use infrared lights, fiber identification, and DNA tracing to turn any Thanksgiving into Mystery Dinner Theater.

Figure out who rubbed one out in the guest shower: was it Uncle Terry? Or is the crime still unsolved!?

**CSIKIT. Jackoff Kit . . . $48.99**
**Questionable. Sometimes doesn't ship.**

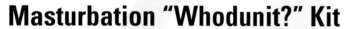

# THE IMAGE SHARPENER

## MACE MY FACE

# Pepper Self-Spray

**Stop yourself before you do something stupid.™**

**Idiot, spray thyself!**
Lob huge loads of bear-
blinding pepper spray into
your own eyes before you
do something you regret!

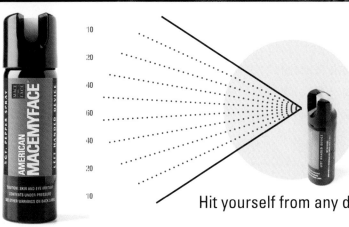

Mace My Face pepper self-spray is a highly toxic blend of chemicals that will send a message from your eyes to your brain: stop what you are doing NOW.

**MACEMYFACE. Pepper Self-Spray . . . $12.99**

Hit yourself from any distance.

# THE IMAGE SHARPENER

## Drive Away Your Guilty Conscience with Our $12.00 Hybrid Magnet

This affordable hybrid emblem will "convert" your gas guzzler into a fuel-efficient vehicle. The authentic-looking badge sticks to the back of your Ferrari, SUV, or Winnebago to make you look like a real friend of the Earth.

**HYBRMG. Hybrid Magnet . . . $12.00**

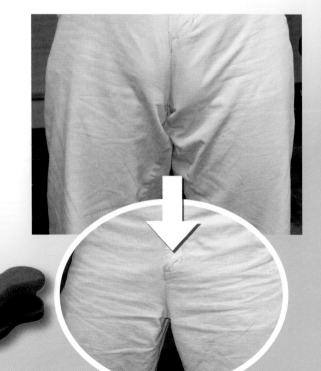

## Camel Toe Eraser

Ever hear someone yell, "Hey Glen: You've got front-butt"? Finally, a solution to a problem that has been dogging people and male band teachers for 60,000 years—camel toe. Those jeans are meant to hide what you've got, not split it in two and paint it blue. Our camel toe eraser, an ultra-modern foam wedge, is a crack filler that is guaranteed to turn your camel toe back into a hoof again!

**CMLTOE. Camel Toe Eraser . . . . $59.99**

## THE IMAGE SHARPENER

## AbMaster Potty Blaster™

The average dad spends exactly one-half of his life on the toilet. And while going to the bathroom is a great way to lose weight, it doesn't build muscle. Until now. Sculpt washboard abs while you take care of business.

**WRKTDMP. Exercise Potty . . . $899.88**

## Temper-Pedic™ Casket

Honor the memory of your loved ones with memory foam. You can even throw an egg at this NASA approved space-cushion technology and the egg will not break! There is no reason to buy this product.

**EZDETH. Temper-Pedic™ Casket . . . $4,884.88**

# THE IMAGE SHARPENER

## "I Give Up" Office Chair

There's no hope of you getting any work done. You're just going to surf the Internet, call your friends, etc. Our ergonomic "I Give Up" chair renders both your body and mind completely useless.

**IGVUP. No-Work Chair . . . $1,095.00**

## SnoGlobe Safe

Keep your SnoGlobes safe! Don't let a thief rob you of the very thing that makes you *you*: your oh-so-precious SnoGlobes.

**SNGLBSF. SnoGlobe Safe . . . $598.00**

## THE STATUETORY
Meeting and Exceeding Your Home Statue Needs

## Garden Emoti-Gnomes

You're a guy, so feelings are hard to talk about. NOT ANYMORE! Show them how you really feel with these quiet loner gnomes for the garden. At the next barbeque, just point and say, "I feel like that."

**CRYSTU. Sad Gargoyle Emoti-Gnome . . . $299.99 ea.**

I feel like *that.*

## THE STATUETORY
Meeting and Exceeding Your Home Statue Needs

## The Lion-Mouth Pee Shower

Pee will come pouring and spilling down on your friends from the maw of this hand-crafted maned beauty from Northern Italy.

The technology is beautifully simple: You get behind the lion and spray into a hole. They stand below and get positively drenched!

Bingo!

**LNPEE. Lion-Mouth Pee Shower . . . $288.99 Dirty. Bad.**

## Large-load model!

**Dirty. Bad. Worse . . . $388.99**

## The Three Veterinarians of Nazareth

In ancient times these beast-healers gamboled about the countryside, laying hands upon sick flocks. Here we see Japeth and Magog looking on as Togarmah nurses a lamb back to consciousness with his own man-breast! Sculpted in terra cotta by artist/seer Darryn Steegan, this homage to the first veterinarians will make you swell up with pride.

**VETSTU. Veterinarian Figurines . . . $18.88**

## THE STATUETORY
### Meeting and Exceeding Your Home Statue Needs

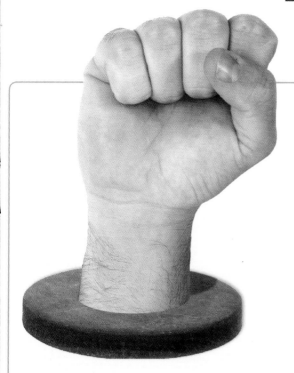

## White Chocolate Black-Power Fist

Commemorate the 1968 Mexico City Olympics with this Black Power fist, stunningly re-rendered in white chocolate!

**EBNYIVRY. White Chocolate Black-Power Fist . . . $45.88**

*"If I'd been there, and been black, I'd have been with you, brother."*
**—Ross McCall, Tennis Pro**

## Abe Lincoln as You've Never Seen Him Before!

Beardless, hatless, and wearing pearls! Yum! Hand-poured in delicious white chocolate, this bust shows our most complex president during his freshman year at university: the log-cabin university of life!

**DRGPRZ. Edible Abe Woman Head . . . $89.00**

## THE STATUETORY
Meeting and Exceeding Your Home Statue Needs

# Memorial to the Unknown Stoner

Remember the dude who gave you a joint at the Phish show? What about that surfer that used to crack you up in drawing class? There are so many stoners that don't get credit for helping people, and this memorial fixes that problem—big time. Hand-carved in soapstone from the Bisbee mines, this six-foot-tall pot pipe will add a magical glow to your home and garden.

**BIGPIP. Giant Pot Pipe . . . $499.00**

# Ancient Retard

Legend has it that King Menouch III got his rock crocked by a longboat oar in A.D. 107. This giant stone head captures him at the moment of impact. The king went on to rule for eight years, twice as long as his father before him. This faux-granite sculpture will keep watch over your estate.

*"Use King 'Tard to guard your yard!"* ™

**ANCRTRD. Ancient Retard Sculpture . . . $139.99**

# diversitopia
exploiting difference since the late '70s

## Black "Friend" Photo

Prove that you've got a diverse peer group with this photo of you and your black "friend" Edward. Tape your face on this pre-framed photo to say, "I get an 'A' in the racism department."

**BLKFRND. Racial Harmony Photo . . . $15.99**

**Fragile. Sensitive.**

## Gay Egg

This is the gayest egg we've ever seen. Buy a bakers dozen and give 'em out on Oscar night!

**GAYEGG. Gay Egg . . . Three-dollar bill**

## Chinese Acne Poster

This reproduction of an ancient Chinese teenager's face shows the key acne zones that release *tuan-xi,* or "healing waves."

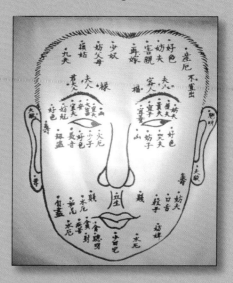

**PMPLFC. Acne Poster . . . $89.76**

## It's Easy!

As easy as one, two . . .
aaggh fuck!

Chess is perhaps America's greatest game. Amazingly, each piece is able to move in a different way. For example, the knight can move in the shape of an "L." And it can go over other pieces. It's unbelievable that a piece could actually go over another piece that's in its way, but it can. Pawns bump into other pieces. The queen goes the farthest, which seems backwards since the king is the most important piece. But that's the way they made the rules of this majestic game.

With our kit, you'll be carving in no time and well on your way to making your first chess set; in fact, many of our customers never carve anything again because it was so great! Included you'll find lush blocks of hard fir and pine ready for carving, an instructional cassette, and our exclusive carving tool, the Gamesman.

You'll never actually have to play this incomprehensible game.

**STITCHS. Carve Your Own Chess Set . . . $54.99**

# Carve Your Own
## *Chess Set*

*Sit down over the board for a romantic evening, and when that special someone says, "I should probably get going," tell them, "I made that whole chess set."*

"Inside every block of wood is a whole mess of different shit that you could carve." —Mark Twain

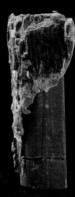

**A FULL SET**
**IN MINUTES**
THEY PRACTICALLY CARVE THEMSELVES

## PROBLETUNITY KNOCKS
### Motivational Posters

### Sailboats at Dawn Poster

Keep the psychological edge over your enemies with this hard-hitting picture of boats in a harbor. A perfect addition to your workout room or psych-out chamber, or use it to cover up the hole that you punched in the wall.

**FCKME. Sunrise Poster . . . $29.00 *plus shipping.***

## PROBLETUNITY KNOCKS
### Motivational Posters

Don't throw another coffee mug at Darryn or Cody and ruin Thanksgiving. When your blood is boiling at all the bullshit you must deal with, just glance up at our inspirational poster to stay focused on your goal.

**FLRPWR. Flower Anger Poster . . . $29.00 (Replacement glass, $19.99)**

Keep it real, and remember that everyone is out to get you. Stick to your program of ab-crunches and reading the dictionary, and you will prevail.

**LKPST. Mountain Lake Motivator . . . $29.00**

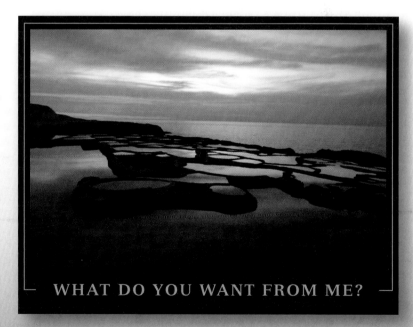

## PROBLETUNITY KNOCKS
### Motivational Posters

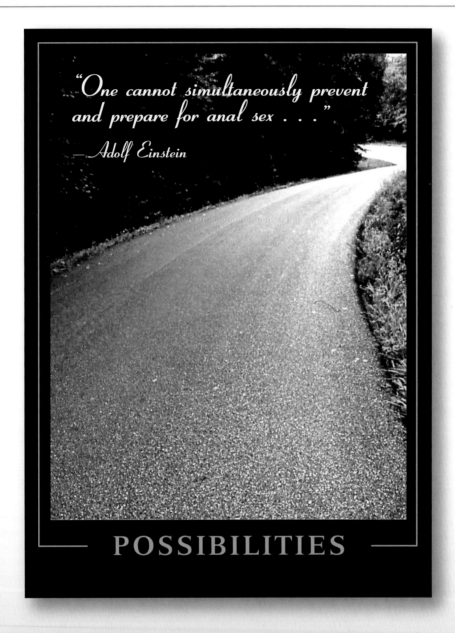

This handsome poster of a road less traveled is adorned with a quote about one of the most famous philosophical conundrums of our time. A real inspiration and thought-provoker; guaranteed to spice up the holiday-dinner conversation.

**ANLSXPST. Philosophy Poster . . . $29.99**

NO GOD

## Atheist Inspirational Poster

A man looked back on his difficult life and imagined two sets of footprints in the sand that at one point became just one set of footprints. "Ah," said the man to himself, "I was walking with the Lord up until that moment, then he abandoned me, and life became hard." Then the Lord came down to the man and said, "I did not abandon you. That is where I took you up and carried you."

Look at this beach: no footprints, no nothin'!

**EXSTNL. "There Is No God" Nature Poster . . . Free**

## Lawsuit Deterrent Posters

As boss of your own company, you've got a lot to deal with. The last thing you want is some employee being all like "I got hurt. I hurt my back," or like, "Oh, I saw you dump toxic something into the water thing." Right? Put these inspirational posters in your break room and help your workers remember a little value called *not crying*.

**NOCOMPU. Worker's Comp/Whistleblower Deterrent Posters . . . $29.99 ea.**

## PROBLETUNITY KNOCKS
### Motivational Posters

**THIS COMPANY IS GOING DOWN!**

Put this terrifying poster in the break room at work, and start the rumors flying. Everyone is thinking it, and now our limited-edition poster will say it, with a ball of flames and a hoseman to really bring the metaphor to life.

**ENRNPS. Failing Business Poster . . . $29.00**

# J. CREWCIFIX
## EXTREME RELIGION SINCE A.D. 33

## Inflatable Portable Ten Commandments Monument

In 2003, Judge Roy Moore was forced to move his own private 5,000-pound Ten Commandments monument out of a government building. 5,000 pounds! Jesus Christ, that's heavy!

That's why we invented our new Inflatable Portable Ten Commandments Monument—within minutes of an atheist, liberal loony judge's ruling to remove it, your Monument can be deflated and folded neatly into the trunk of your Buick. With the money you save on moving costs, you could even start your own titty bar called Hypocri-Titties!

### The Commandments

I
Thou shalt have no other gods before me

II
Thou shalt not make unto thee any graven image

III
Thou shalt not take the name of the LORD thy God in vain

IV
Remember the sabbath day to keep it holy

V
Honour thy father and thy mutha

### Ten Commandments

VI
Thou shalt not kill God

VII
Thou shalt not commit adultery

VIII
steal steal steal

IX
Thou shalt not bear false witness against thy neighbour

X
Thou shalt kill bears

**TENCMD. Inflatable Ten Commandments Monument . . . $125.00**

## Giant Bible!

This humongous Bible is one of our biggest products. Hand-woven and lovingly typeset in traditional sixteenth century "madre de puta" boldface, this Book of God will make you feel faithful and humble. Put it on your rooftop or by the backyard pool to show your neighbors the true size and girth of your faith. Perfect for a vacation home, to remind you that Jesus is there, even when you're puking.

**XXLBBL. Big Bible . . . $899.99**

## J. CREWCIFIX
### EXTREME RELIGION SINCE A.D. 33

## Christian Over-the-Clothes Massage Lotion

Put the "gas" back in massage with our Christian-friendly over-the-clothes lotion. Squirt it all over a sweater, jeans, or T-shirt, instead of naked skin, so that you can lead yourself not into temptation.

**JSSLTN. OTC Lotion . . . $27.99**

# J. CREWCIFIX
## EXTREME RELIGION SINCE A.D. 33

## Tweaker Cross

What better to wear when you are riding someone else's ten-speed across a hot city to get to the pawnshop, or when you are practicing some Kara-te on the interstate at 4:00 A.M. You've been up for days; you are the king; and God has given you a big tip-off about what the landlord is up to. Wear your tweaker cross with pride. You are not Jesus, but no one has to know . . . right, Jesus?

**TWLCRS. Tweaker Cross . . . $179.00**

**Order this with our Tweaker Bike (p. 110)**

## You Know Wutt Beads

These prayer beads are just begging for it. If the creator didn't want these where the sun don't shine, he shouldn't have intelligently designed them to be so butt-ticklingly smooth and brown.

**BCKDRBDS. Smooth Beads . . . $45.99**

Everyone's got nuts,
but not everyone's got the balls to
leave them in Thailand . . .

More leg room. More mixed nuts.
More flights to sex-reassignment surgery destinations than any other airline.

*Tranny World Airlines*
You Are Now Free to Use the Ladies' Room

# Lords and Ladies...
# Here be Softwaire!!

## iPeasant
### The Complete *Renaissance Faire* Solution

*Good Morrow!* You always dress up like King Henry, and Dave assumes the guise of the Merry Wife of Windsor—God knows how many Faires you two have been a-gallavanting to in the old blue van. Now you can map out the Faire circuit, keep notes on costume ideas, and input phone numbers for Buxom Maidens, with iPeasant! Our software is hand-pressed on the finest, softest European deer hide. Jam it into the drive and start trippin'!

* Knockin' Bootz Bar-Wench Finder
* Tights-Bulge Girth Optimizer: Stuff but Don't Overstuff!™
* Fearn to fpeak Olde Englifh!
* Avoid "Faire Babies" with Medieval Rhythm Method
* Turkey leg simulator!!
* "Master of the Phaedog" Flute-tutor

 *Global Faire Finder:* Every faire from Vacaville to Gilroy hand-drawn on virtual parchment maps.

 *Grognometer: Tired of puking in Porta-Potties?* Our Grognometer lets you pace your mead intake based on your medication!

 *Donkey-Wagon Converter:* Tells you how long it would've taken to get there in a donkey wagon instead of a Dodge van.

## iPeasant Ren Faire Planner

| | | |
|---|---|---|
| **IPSNT. iPeasant Ren Faire Planning Software** | . . . | **$99.00** |
| **Virtual Codpiece CD-ROM** | . . . | **$29.00** |
| **Deer Antler Hard Drive** | . . . | **$222.00** |

PESTLE-2-PESTLE

*Gourmet Drugs and Food Since 1998*

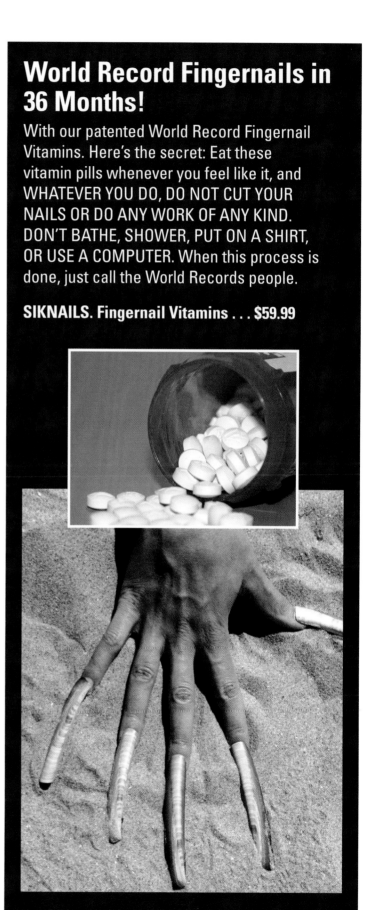

## World Record Fingernails in 36 Months!

With our patented World Record Fingernail Vitamins. Here's the secret: Eat these vitamin pills whenever you feel like it, and WHATEVER YOU DO, DO NOT CUT YOUR NAILS OR DO ANY WORK OF ANY KIND. DON'T BATHE, SHOWER, PUT ON A SHIRT, OR USE A COMPUTER. When this process is done, just call the World Records people.

**SIKNAILS. Fingernail Vitamins . . . $59.99**

## Food Fight of the Month Club

Every month, we send you a basketload of food you can throw at each other while reenacting a historical skirmish to up the "fun ante." Look forward to Vanilla Custard's Last Stand, the Rodney King Crab Riots (pictured), Dessert Storm, or Fondue Vietnam.

Picture busting a bottle of Pellegrino over somebody's back while you are wearing a Winston Churchill waistcoat. It simply could not get any funner.

**FOODFT. Historical Food Fight Baskets . . . $45.00/mo.**

PESTLE-2-PESTLE
*Gourmet Drugs and Food Since 1998*

## Stop Aging Once and for All . . . with Poison!

Forget Botox, Laser Peel, HGH, or face-lifts. Stop the heart with poison, and you'll feel cellular aging grind to a halt! Say goodbye to frown lines, acne blemishes, liver spots, warts—poison wipes them out for good! You will stay the same age. Forever. Guaranteed.

**PSNCLB. Poison Anti-Aging Kit . . . $49.99/mo.**

## Dorm Room "Plant of the Month" Subscription Service

Spice up your son or daughter's bland habitat with some vibrant greens. SkyMaul will send your little B or C student a different flowering plant every month to add color, life, and pizzazz to winter quarter, sophomore slump, or Thursday Study Munch. Plus, they learn how to take care of something!

**POTCLB. Care Package . . . $149.99/mo.**

You tested positive for 😞

## Break it to them tastefully with our
# Medical Test Results Fortune Cookies™

Being a doctor is literally nine times as hard as any other job. And the hardest part is lying to a patient about their illness. Now you don't have to. With our Medical Test Results Fortune Cookies, you can give your patients a fortune cookie that really does tell them their future instead of revealing something stupid like, "You will have good luck in business." These test-result cookies are fun, interactive, and low carb.

Imagine this interaction:

PATIENT: "What did the test say?"
DOCTOR: "I don't know. Would you like a fortune cookie?"
PATIENT: "Yum . . . Oh, crap."

See? Easy.

**MEDCOK. Medical Test Results Fortune Cookies™ . . . $18.99/dozen**
**Sugar Free "You Have Diabetes" Cookies . . . $11.99/dozen**

## Tomorrow's Garage Sale
**Filling up your home, office, and storage areas**

### The *Moby Dick* Hamster Coffin

Send Freckles out just like Queequeg.
Perfect for a burial at sea—or down the toilet!

This hand-carved mini-coffin is etched with "primitive" asterisks and tick tack toes, just like the godless savages would have used in the Middle Ages, when Herman Melville wrote his famous time-travel story.

*"Smacks of authenticity."*
—Mo Lee, Ph.D.

**MBYDK. Moby Dick Hamster Coffin . . . $39.99**

### *Da Vinci Code* Decoder Ring

Spoiler warning: Da Movie sucks! Buy this for $2.00 and call it a night!

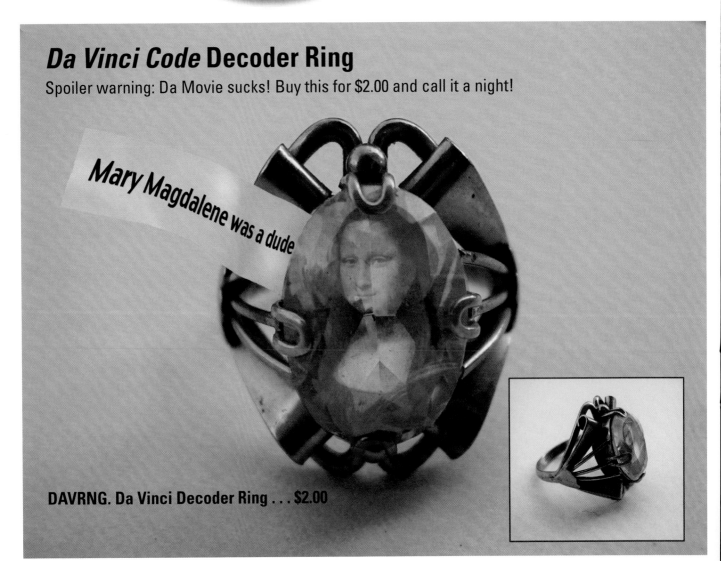

Mary Magdalene was a dude

**DAVRNG. Da Vinci Decoder Ring . . . $2.00**

## This Australian Thinking Hat Will Help You Figure Out What to Major In!

What do you want to do with your life? Help people? Make money? Or start your own thing? Sometimes it feels like too much freedom can lead to paralysis? Put on your shell necklace, pop on our mesh philosopher-cowboy hat, and go for a walk—off campus!

**AUSHAT. Indecision Hat; one size fits all . . . $29.00**

## Stoner Welding Kit

Get high, and get welding! This stoner welding kit comes with a face mask, a bag of green bud, and a Led Zeppelin CD.

**STNWLD. Stoner Welding Kit . . . $60–$120\***

*\*Depending on Market Value*

# Tomorrow's Garage Sale

Filling up your home, office, and storage areas

## Nazi Grandpa Locator

Grandpa Helmut sort of disappeared after 1945. Now you can teach your kids about his likely whereabouts!

Holding a Guinness Book Record for how huge it is, this giant wall map lights up with the hiding places of your relatives. The next time they say, "Where's Grandpa again?" you can point to the map and say, "I *told* you, Argentina. He did a bad thing."

Connect your kids to history . . . and to their *Großvater.*

**NZIMAP. Giant Wall Map . . . $99.99**

## Eye Pillow

You can throw all of those lame little lavender pouches in the G-A-R-B-A-G-E. Our eye pillow is 100 percent American: big, strong, and in your face! Your worries will drift away as you remove your shirt, step on our patented eye pillow step stool, and brain-dive your way down into Dreamsylvania.

**BDHAL. Eye Pillow Grande . . . $29.00**
**Eye Pillow Step Stool . . . $59.99**
**Eye Pillow Stand . . . $19.99**

*May cause back strain and nightmares.*

## Tomorrow's Garage Sale

Filling up your home, office, and storage areas

## French Postman's Love Barge

The French are famous for two things: wine and bread and having sex. Three things, sorry. And French postmen, apparently, are uncircumcised so they can love, love, love without losing the important sensations that the foreskin provides.

**FRNCHBK. French Postbike . . . $918.00**

## MeeMaw and PeePaw House-Cluttering Trinket

Every time Grandma has a vodka stumble, one of these things comes crashing off the shelves.

**CRMCSHT. Porcelain Crap . . . $49.99**

## Tribal Bowling Ball Carrier

There is a bowling ball inside our beautiful, easy-to-smash terra cotta carrier. Break it out, and break your friend's face on the big wooden lane of truth!

**BWLBLL. Bowling Ball Jug . . . $99.00**

## Tomorrow's Garage Sale

Filling up your home, office, and storage areas

## "Don't Ask, Don't Tell" Medal

Reward Mom and Dad for minding their own business with this Frankleton Mint beauty. They can wear it to the gas station, and when someone asks what it's for, they can say, "I don't know, my son gave it to me ... I think he's gay ... or it had something to do with us letting him be gay?"

**GAYSRV. Don't Ask Medal . . . $45.27**

## Commemorative Freedom Medallion

Celebrate American Freedom with this special commemorative medallion. Featuring our country's founder on one side and an eagle in a tree on the back, each quarter-sized sculpture is issued by the real U.S. Mint and stamped with a date and a famous quote by Jesus.

**FRDMCON. U.S. Freedom Coin . . . $5.99/ea.**

## Tomorrow's Garage Sale
Filling up your home, office, and storage areas

## Say Good-bye to Your Coins Forever With Our Sink-Mounted Change Disposal

No one likes change—especially loose change! Now you can kiss your pennies, nickels, and dimes good-bye . . . and good luck. This sink-mounted change disposal will grind handfuls of coins or freedom medallions into drain-friendly powder, and when coins are ground up, their value disappears from the world, so your other money is worth more.

**CHNGSNK. Coin disposal . . . $344.99**

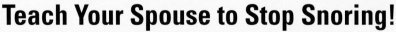

## Teach Your Spouse to Stop Snoring!

This antique cannon fires blanks—but makes a REAL sound that says, "Will you please please please please shut the fuck up or move to the living room?!"

Show them you mean business.

**SPSCN. Snore-buster Civil War Cannon . . . $5,666.00**
Illegal in AL, AZ, BF, CA, CT, DE, IL, FL, GA, IL, IN, KY

## Oops, this is my house!

## Home Beluga-quarium!

Nobody'll say you didn't have a whale of a time building a beluga-quarium in your very own living room! Smash one wall down with a sledgehammer, and pop this nifty whale box right in! Guests will marvel: "What the fuck did you do, Trey?"

This kit includes everything you need to be the talk of the neighborhood.

**WHILKS. Beluga-quarium . . . $Two paychecks**
**Whale CPR Kit . . . $555.00**

## Racial Globe Toaster

This globe is also a toaster! Press any country, and your toast will toast to the shade of its inhabitants' skin! From Swedish white to Korean lightly browned to Nigerian well done. Fun!

This is the first and last racial globe toaster you will ever buy.

**RCLGLB. Racial Globe Toaster . . . $49.99**

Oops, this is my house!

## Louis XIV Fart Chair

This chair will take any fart and swallow it without a peep. You can just sit there and smile, and no one will even know what's happening until later in the day.

**DPRDCHR. Fart Chair . . . $299.99**
**Replacement Cushion . . . $109.99**

## "I Have a Dream" Step Stool

Reach for the stars with this little ladder that was inspired by civil rights leader Martin Luther King Jr.'s "I Have a Dream" speech.

*"I have a dream . . ."* — Martin Luther King Jr.

**MLKSTP. Reach for the Stars Stool . . . $99.00**

## "Twin Towers" Media Storage Center

Commemorate the tragedy of 9/11 as you organize hundreds of your CDs and DVDs in two versatile "Twin Towers." Never forget what the terrorists did to Freedom, and never forget where you put your "Lion King" DVD—it's in the Twin Towers!

**WTCRCK. Not funny . . . $129.99**

# *NASCAR* Stepdad
### Don't flip out!

## HUMMER 5 is Finally Here!

Our special "We're sorry, We fucked up" edition puts you where the power is! Four-wheel drive (not all at the same time) and plenty of room for you and . . . Oh, God, there's hardly any more oil left. Hopefully the Rapture will come soon.

**WRSORY. Hummer 5 . . . $199,899.67**

## Hot Dog Shooter

This nifty meat gun combines two of America's favorite hobbies—hot dogs and guns—into one fun shooter! Works great with our Hot-Dog Catcher (page 108). Makes a perfect gift for a loved one that likes to pump out a dog far.

**HTDOGN. Hot Dog Shooter . . . $89.99**

# NASCAR Stepdad
## Don't flip out!

## Uncle Terry's Shit-Head Sled

Get some eggnog up in you and just have a great time on the slopes with Uncle Terry's four-man sled. Hand-welded (by hand) in Pukaibah County, CA. Passenger seat reclines.

Nowhere to put feet until they've been rammed up your ass by gravity and alcohol.

**DTHSLEIGH. Shit-Head Sled . . . $699.98**

## Uncle Terry's Bullshit Bullet Boat

Your mom's older brother is an asshole, and he thinks you and the rest of the cousins like to be whipped around on this inflatable raft.

Well, you don't, and in fact you're really scared and worried you will snap your neck. Plus, no one is mentioning that Terry is on his second twelve-pack.

Just stay focused, try to do well in school, go to college, and you can leave all these fuckwads behind.

**DRNKBTR. Uncle Terry's Bullshit Bullet Boat . . . $98.99**

# Make Your Golden Years Even More Golden With Our Metal Detector Walking Aids

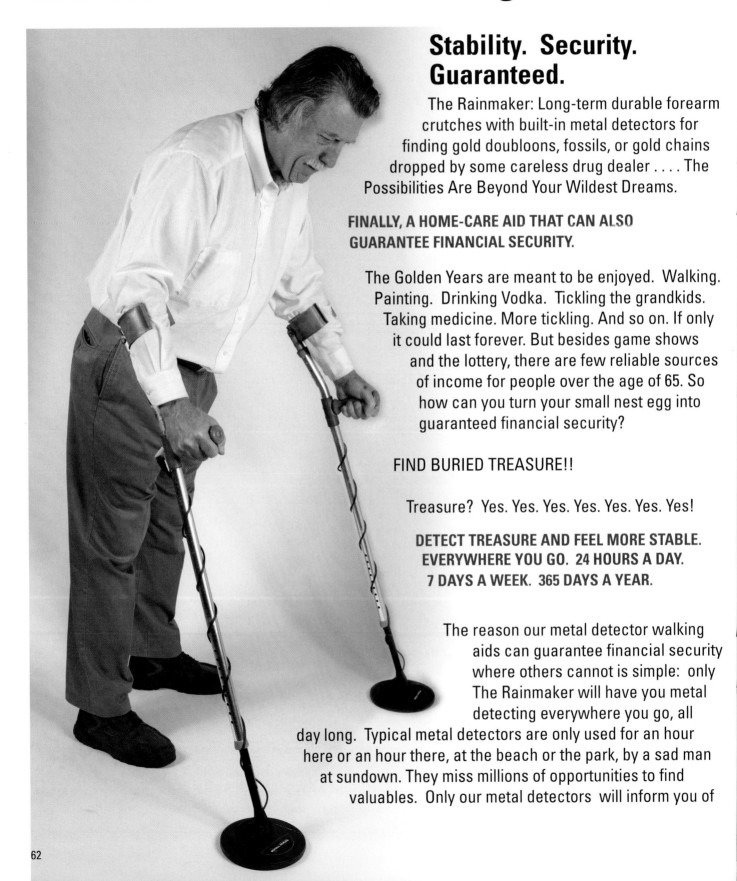

## Stability. Security. Guaranteed.

The Rainmaker: Long-term durable forearm crutches with built-in metal detectors for finding gold doubloons, fossils, or gold chains dropped by some careless drug dealer .... The Possibilities Are Beyond Your Wildest Dreams.

**FINALLY, A HOME-CARE AID THAT CAN ALSO GUARANTEE FINANCIAL SECURITY.**

The Golden Years are meant to be enjoyed. Walking. Painting. Drinking Vodka. Tickling the grandkids. Taking medicine. More tickling. And so on. If only it could last forever. But besides game shows and the lottery, there are few reliable sources of income for people over the age of 65. So how can you turn your small nest egg into guaranteed financial security?

FIND BURIED TREASURE!!

Treasure? Yes. Yes. Yes. Yes. Yes. Yes. Yes!

**DETECT TREASURE AND FEEL MORE STABLE. EVERYWHERE YOU GO. 24 HOURS A DAY. 7 DAYS A WEEK. 365 DAYS A YEAR.**

The reason our metal detector walking aids can guarantee financial security where others cannot is simple: only The Rainmaker will have you metal detecting everywhere you go, all day long. Typical metal detectors are only used for an hour here or an hour there, at the beach or the park, by a sad man at sundown. They miss millions of opportunities to find valuables. Only our metal detectors will inform you of

the presence of valuable metals at the Social Security Office, restaurants, hospital waiting rooms, or tour buses.

## WHEREVER YOU ARE. WHATEVER YOU FIND IS YOURS. PERIOD.

Can a walker make you money? No. Can a wheelchair or electric scooter make you money? No way! The Rainmaker is the only mobility aid that pays for itself. The AARP has even called them "slot machines on sticks."

## EXPERTS SAY METAL DETECTING IS THE ONLY GUARANTEED MONEY-MAKER THIS CENTURY.

Metal detecting can't lose.  It can only win. Uri Volvchenchek, a former economist with the World Council, estimates that in the next ten years the world will double in weight due to buried treasure. Likely.  Guaranteed.

## IT'S ALSO THE BEST FOREARM CRUTCH MADE:  DARTH VADER AND THE SECRET OF STABILO-PADS.

The Rainmaker is also a great walking aid in its own right because of sturdy construction and the patented metal-detecting Stabilo-pads. These pads double the stability of the crutch by duplicating the futuristic technology invented by Darth Vader and used effectively on the feet of Imperial Walkers during the battle of Hoth. Stability.  Peace of Mind.  Military/Space-Walking Technology.  Tested on Hoth.

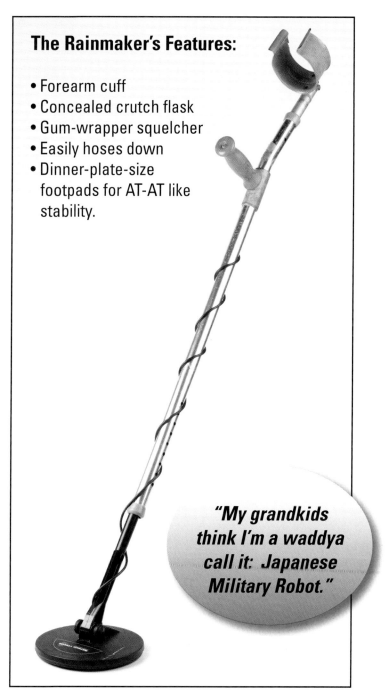

### The Rainmaker's Features:

- Forearm cuff
- Concealed crutch flask
- Gum-wrapper squelcher
- Easily hoses down
- Dinner-plate-size footpads for AT-AT like stability.

*"My grandkids think I'm a waddya call it:  Japanese Military Robot."*

**RTRMTN. The Rainmaker Retirement Crutch/Metal Detectors . . . $999.00**
**Jewelry Melter . . . $19.00**

*Toys for demanding kids...*

## Transforkshire Terrier

This incredible kids' toy transforms from a dog to a robot—and back again! Who knows where the dog goes—probably to the fifth dimension or beyond!—but Arlo and Trisha's eyes will pop out of their heads when they see their lovable Yorkshire terrier change from a trembling titmouse into a death-dealing cyber-bot.

**TRNFRDG. Robot-Canine . . . $324.99**

**New!**
**Transforhuahua**
**$324.99**

# Happy crap you can buy from a plane!

*Toys for demanding kids...*

## Cute Lindbergh Bear (Pro-Hitler)

He's cute, he's sexy, he's a national hero! He's also a tiny bit pro-Hitler, too! Which is a super downer! Your little loved ones will adore this cuddly aviator. Comes with a furry Service Cross of the German Eagle, the medal that Lindbergh got from Hermann Goering, the head of the Luftwaffe! Oops! Cute!

**NZIBR. Lindbergh Doll . . . $99.99**

## *Apocalypse Now* Talking Kitten

This adorable mechanical kitten is loaded with classic lines from *Apocalypse Now*! Amuse your friends and enemies when you pull the string and hear it say:

*"My mission is to make it up into Cambodia. There's a Green Beret Colonel up there who's gone insane. I'm supposed to kill him."*

*"I love the smell of Napalm in the morning."*

*"Never get out of the boat! Never get out of the boat!"*

A great cocktail party ice breaker.

**KRTZKITN. Apocalypse Now Kitten Toy . . . $39.99**

*The horror, the horror!*

*Toys for demanding kids…*

## "Tickle Me Oswald" Kiddy Book Depository Model

Teach your kids about the Kennedy conspiracy with our fun collectable model of the Dallas book depository. Let your little ones ask, "Daddy, how in the hell did he hit him from there, three times?!" You can say, "He didn't, Tim. And please don't say 'hell.'"

**GRSYKNL. JFK Toy Building . . . $45.99**

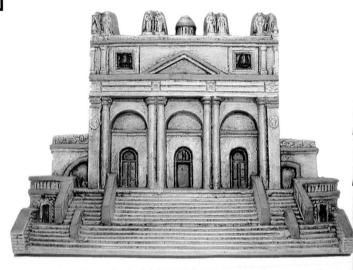

## Li'l Tagger™ Graffiti/Muralist Set

Imagine your child creating incredible scenes of artwork ten stories high: dragons, words, whatever, all beautifully painted on other people's property.

To be a great urban artist, you need a bad attitude and a can of spray paint, for starters. Let your kid write his or her name on everything, including train cars, roadsigns, trucks, newspaper racks, and store windows, with our "Li'l Tagger"™ kit.

Show the little stranger you do know what's hip and rebellious.

**SPRDWN. Kids' Graffiti Set . . . $78.99**

*Toys for demanding kids . . .*

## Our Safest Electric Jungle Gym

This electrically heated Jungle Gym was rigorously tested by fire experts, and still—look what happened. It should be fine. What are the chances of this happening twice?

**FRPRF. Safest Jungle Gym . . . $599.99**

## Gladio-Bopper Pool and Sharks

Let's face a fact here: your kid is a totally unrecognized champion/gentleman/scholar/athlete. He just hasn't found a way to express *any* of those qualities.

Give him a chance to knock the starting QB into a shark pool. The set includes two Bopper Battle Staffs.™

**FMBMPR. Social Darwin Gene Pool . . . $159.99**
**Sharks . . . $14,000.00 ea.**
**Tube socks . . . $12.99**

## Throwing Soaps

These star-shaped bath oils are just like metal Ninja throwing stars, except they won't cost you an arm and a leg when your little Spencer beans a dork in the head. All the anger, twice the cleanliness.

**SOPCHKR. Soaps . . . $89.99**

## WhadjaGITme?
*Toys for demanding kids...*

## Fat Alcoholic Neddy Bear

This silly fun reality bear lies on his back just like Uncle Dick. Pull a string and listen to Neddy Bear say:

*"Where's my pants?"*
*"The damn 'Niners, fuckin'..."*
*"Oooh, here I go again!"*

**WSTDBR. Neddy Bear ... $49.99**

## Pre-1933 Micky Mouse

"Yuck ... but in a cute way" is how your lucky son or daughter or little uncle will feel about this piece of American Cartoonamagraphic history. Handmade and strictly limited to however many we sell, this sturdy, funny little trash rat will cause joy of the person who receives it. What little tricks is Micky up to now? Eating something? Digging a hole? Like a real mouse? Yes.

**NZIMCKY. Vintage Micky ... $99.99**

## Heavy Duty Leapfrog Suits

Here's two people having a blast playing one of the world's funnest games: leapfrog. These suits are double reinforced, so no more scrapes, bruises, boners, or groaners. Huzzah!

**TRTLPRTY. Safe, fun leapfrog suits ... $89.99**

*Toys for demanding kids...*

## Homeschooler Afterschool Snacks

Eli, Josiah, and Rain deserve a break. They've been studying for the SATs by reading the Old Testament, learning about sharks and King Tut, and staring at the spot where the TV used to be. But it's too early for a whole bowl of millet, and yoghurt is poisoned with sugar. Show your little genius he's too special for public school with our amazing raw-food popsicles. Comes in packages of twelve.

**Cool Cucumber, Literate Lettuce, Brilliant Banana, Technical Tomato, or Lazarus Lemon.**

**VEGSCL. Homeschool Popsicles . . . $10.99**

## Karate Belt-ganizer

Organize your kid's karate belts, or let him do it himself. But he's going to have to learn the right way to do it, so you show him and he watches. When he gets older, he can put the belts in there himself, but for now you do it, because this rack is expensive.

**BLTRK. Obi-ganizer . . . $88.00**

## "The Way I See Myself" Stoner Trophy

Other people see you as selfish and irritable. Maybe they don't value your future plans or the fact that you are 100 percent virile. Our stoner trophy will always be there to remind you that you are a Golgoth inside—a writhing, totally ripped demon who is trapped under layers of junk-food-induced lard that isn't your fault.

**STNRSLF. Trophy . . . $45.99**

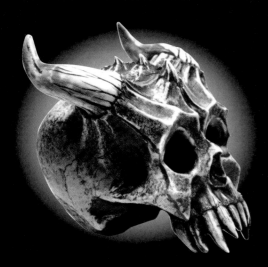

## Cry for Help Object

Lonely, scared, having confusing feelings about you know what? Just take our new "Cry for Help Object" to the school nurse, and you will get to go to one of those sweet wilderness rehab programs.

**C4HELP. Attention-getting Skull . . . $99.00**

## "I Am a Dangerous Nerd" Kit

Throwing stars, metal dog paw, and knife-comb combine to spell one thing: who cares about football?! I can throw these things into a dart board; and they're called Shuriken, not throwing stars, jock!

**NRDPCK. Weapons of Destruction . . . $87.88**

# KNICKERS 'N KICKERS
Celebrating the world of knee-pants, shoes, sandals, shorts, or whatever

## Our Worst-Selling Motocross Boots!

These hand-sewn motocross boots have gel packs built into the heel and toe, and special SureGrip sole pads are supposed to glue your feet to the pegs. The shoes have been a real albatross in our stockroom and we cannot sell them.

**PLEASE. Motocross Boots . . . $17.99, or pay what you can**

## Pre-9/11 Fantasy Slippers

Click your heels together three times and be transported to October 2000: pre-Florida, pre-9/11, pre-Iraq, pre-Katrina. You'll still have to go through all that stuff, but it won't start happening for a couple of months.

**TRRCLGS. 10/00 Slippers . . . $59.99**

## Llama Legs!

Spice up any two-legged llama, guanaco, or vicuña with these furry little spindly treasures, or add them to a complete llama for six legs of Andes-pumping, pack-hauling pleasure. Buy four sets, poke 'em into a watermelon, and voilà: silly summer fruit spider!

Inhumane. May not work.

**03984. Piernas de llama . . . $750.00**

# KNICKERS 'N KICKERS
Celebrating the world of knee-pants, shoes, sandals, shorts, or whatever

## Buddhist Racing Sandals

Beat the other monks up the stairs with our patented Dharma-sole racing thongs. Leave them in the dust as you ascend the steps to enlightenment and sweet, sweet victory!

**ZENSOL. Monk Sandals with Dharma Racing Sole . . . $55.99**

Toasting the role of alcohol in our nation's economy

## Business 'n Spirits

## "Cat's in the Cradle" Flask

An elegant business flask that will remind you of who you're doing it all for. Engraved with the lyrics to Harry Chapin's hit song:

*"When you comin' home, Dad,
I don't know when . . ."*

The quote is inscribed upside down so you can read it mid-gulp!

**CIKMM. Flask . . . $89.00**

## Some New Golf Clubs!

Are you a "golf-a-holic"? Hooray! Treat yourself to these beauties and blow your worries up the wind.

**FHK. Clubs .
. . $600.00**

## D.U.I. Mask

Nothing does the talking at a D.U.I. checkpoint better than this bullman face. Have a couple big highballs at Harrah's and get on the main road wearing this special mask. When the Man asks, "Have you had anything to drink tonight?" you will say in a deep voice you have never heard before, "CAN'T GET ME, PIG, I'M BELZONOOR THE DEMON PRINCE!"

**BLMN. D.U.I. Mask . . . $40.00
(May involve soul hijacking. Can also be used as a banana holder.)**

73

# VICE PRESIDENT OF YOUR OWN LIFE

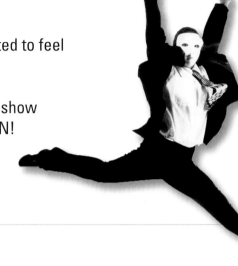

## The "Phantom of the Office"

We agree with you that even casual Fridays have started to feel downright stuffy!

This "free to be me" mask, blazer, and tights outfit will show everyone in the mailroom that you're serious about FUN!

**PNTMOF. Work Mask and Tights . . . $222.00**
**Pointy Shoes . . . Sold Out**

## The "Motel Buddy"

### Executive Companion Sock

Motels are for two things: HBO is one of them. Discreet, sturdy, and comfortable, our executive Motel Buddy has the look, feel, and weight of a regular non-humping sock.

**DRTYSCK. Motel Buddy . . . $1.99**

## Finally, a Real Dolphin for only $14,000!

Realize your childhood dream of owning your own dolphin! Tell all the naysayers to suck it!

**DLPHNU. Real Dolphin . . . $14,000.00**
**(Shipping is tricky.)**
**Dolphin pool . . . You're on your own.**

# VICE PRESIDENT OF YOUR OWN LIFE

## "Jesus Talks Business" Audio Books

Let the Messiah help save your failing company. Three CDs with ten unbelievable lectures from one of history's great management philosophers.

Lectures include:

- Hirin' and Firin'
- Jokin' and Tokin'
- Show Me the Money!
- I got the spice, you bring the sauce / You can kiss my ass, you funky boss.

Read by Ralph Fiennes.

**JSSBZZ. Jesus Talkin' . . . $99.00**

**Company Sales**

Legend: Pray, Pray, Pray

(Bar chart: Sales vs Business — 1st Qtr, 2nd Qtr, 3rd Qtr, 4th Qtr; y-axis 0–90)

## Bean Safe

Beans are the cheapest object in the world, but that trend simply can't last.

Store your beans in our patented new bean safe and finally get some peace of mind. Not even you will know the combination, so you can rest easy, sleeping throughout the day and surfing the net at night.

**PINTOSAFE. Bean Safe . . . $569.99**

# VICE PRESIDENT OF YOUR OWN LIFE

## Job Seeker Decoy Kit

Place this coffee, newspaper, and half-eaten scone out on the breakfast table, then head off to the riverboat casino! When she wakes up, you'll look like little Mr. Business Man, off a' job hunting. Scone and latte contain the same plastics they use for sushi displays, which means you can reuse this ruse until you hit the motherlode in Keno. Your number will come up—it's just Math-a-Matics.

**FKMFN. Spouse Faker . . . $89.99**

## Narcotics Pay/Owe Ledger Book

Jimmy came over last night (or was it Tuesday night?) and got a "sample" and Sady owes you for an eightball or was it a quarter? Trying to remember all of these little transactions when it all runs together into a numbing phosphorous blur and your plans are finally coming together and you almost have enough saved to go legit but you did borrow some of your own stash and um um your teeth are numb and what were we saying? Where the fuck's that rat Jimmy?

**SCRBLBK. Drug Ledger . . . $45.00**

# The fastest way to learn a Middle Earth or Deep Space language. Guaranteed.

At long last, a bright new way to learn that's got people blithering all over the world. Using the highly lauded Golden Stream method, our CD-ROM course will pump a new language into you without you having to read dictionaries, write on chalkboards, or deal with the whole "repeat after me, I'm a French teacher, so I'm better than you" vibe.

| Quenya | Klingon | Rohirric | Valarin | Vulcan | Taliska | Computer | Romulan | Huttese |
|--------|---------|----------|---------|---------|---------|----------|---------|---------|
| Ork | Kobold | Entish | Hobbitish | Scottish | Westron | Goblinian | Sindarin | Ryl |
| Telerin | Ewok | Khuzdul | Wookie | Bachi | Adunaic | R2 | Precioussss | Taun-Taun |

Putting together over a billion pictures and recordings of people who actually speak these languages in their everyday lives, our system duplicates the feeling of being a baby, learning how to talk all over again, with a pant leg full of dribbled sweet potato. One-hundred percent superior to any other nonexistent language learning program or your money back. That's it. No joke.

 **Hearing** – Sword of the Stone uses real people speaking these actual languages the way they would around their castle, starship cruiser, or swamp—so you develop a natural style.

 **Reading** – Special drills help you read by showing the objects next to the words. Genius, Huh? It's like an encyclopedia in a TV.

 **Talking** – The computer hears what you say and communicates to a creature on Naboo, to see if you're right, then flunks you.

 **Writing** – Special drills test how well you can copy what you hear, like, "Ja Bo da yo waka thermal detonator."

## Sword of the Stone

**Each Completely User-Friendly Kit Includes:**
- CD-ROM course with twelve drills in each of 941 lessons.
- Pictures, lists, lessons, and drills for each thing.

Sword of The Stone Vol. 1 . . . $235.00
Sword of The Stone Vol. 2 . . . $275.00

**BEST DEAL YET:** BOTH VOLUMES . . . $941.00

Includes Ork Lunch Etiquette Book, *I Believe That's My Flesh You Are Eating . . .*

## www.skymaul.com

"The next time someone asks me if I speak Bachi, I'll say 'Jerusha-blatz!'"
— *Geoff Sobelle, École Jock la Cock*

"Beep-beep, brrrrp, beep beep. Guess who that is? Me! Droppin' some old school R2 at my captors."
— *Jacob Goldstein, Pukaibah Corr. Inst.*

## Shemail
### Doodads for Ladies

## Backyard PMS Bungalow

Designed by women for women, this sturdy straw PMS bungalow can take it. A perfect place to eat a pint of Chunky Munky™ and throw stuff at the walls.

And the beautiful wood and straw hut will enhance the natural beauty of your yard.

**PMBNGLW. Build-it-Yourself**
**PMS Bungalow . . . $4,448.87**

***Our Bodies, Our Huts: A Herstory of***
***Thatched Roof Dwellings . . . $27.99***

*Includes mood log and ice cream!*

## Heavy Petter

## "Purple = Rabies" Dog Tester Kit

For a dog, rabies is worse than herpes. Stop worrying and test your pet—before it's too late. Spray one squirt of our exclusive patented "Purple = Rabies" formula on your dog: if he turns purple, he has rabies. If he comes out any other color besides purple, he does not have rabies. If he turns purple and his leg turns blue, then he has rabies of the leg.

Heavy Petter's
**PURPLE
=
RABIES**
24 fl. oz

A MUST-HAVE anywhere squirrels, bats, or cats are found!! Don't let this happen to your beloved dog!!

**"Purple = Rabies" Dog Tester**

**Find out. NOW . . . $19.95**

**55-Gallon  Ranch Sprayer . . . $15.89**
**Neighbor-Dog Distance Nozzle . . . $8.00**

Non-rabies (Safe)          Rabies (Danger)[1]

3x magnification

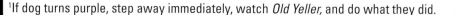

[1]If dog turns purple, step away immediately, watch *Old Yeller,* and do what they did.

# Heavy Petter

. . . pushing animal product on people.

## Sky Monkees™

Remember Sea Monkees? These are the same, but they are funny cute Sky Monkees!™

Comes with a Sky Monkee FunHut™—loaded with sweet, sticky MonkeeNectar.™

**SMNKEE. 100 Sky Monkees™ . . . $88.99**
**Sky Monkee FunHut™ . . . $99.00**
**"Wasp My Tears Away" Herbal Sting Poultice . . . $11.00**

*Just4Kids!*

*Dangerous. Not for kids.

. . . pushing animal product on people.

## Heavy Petter

## Build Your Own Mermaid! (not shown)

With this do-it-yourself home mermaid builder, the sky is the limit. You've got the intelligence and the free time, now scissor together a super-hot fantasy friend.

**TRSNFDG. Mermaid Kit . . . $699.99. Illegal.**

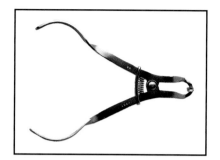

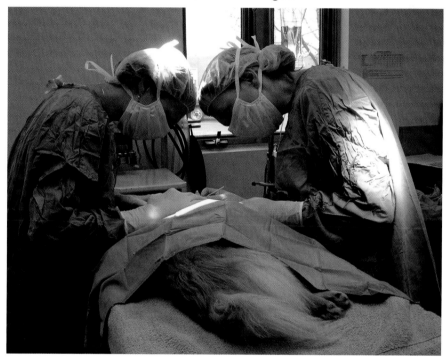

## Scarlet Dog Letters

Show people that your pet did something bad.

P = poo eater

L = leg humper

This time-tested motivational system dates back to the dogs on the Mayflower.

**HSTRPRN. Dog Letters . . . $16.99 ea.**

# Heavy Petter
### . . . pushing animal product on people.

*Tiger-nomic Stretching Log*

## Tiger Arm Extender

It's a well-known fact that a tiger's arms shrink with age. Don't let your pet become the laughing stock of the animal kingdom. With our patented Tiger-nomic stretching log, your beast will achieve arm lengths of over 1,000 percent!

This is so awesome; you really just have to buy it to believe it!

**TGRARM. Tiger Arm Extender . . . $899.99**

**Too short!** Tigers rely on long arms to catch the prey they need. Don't let this happen to your tiger!

## Train Your Vicious Dog from the Air

Our suspension rope and hip-clip feed bag keep you out of Frankenstein the Mauler's bite range. Throw the treats down and yell your commands from a safe distance.

**DAMDOG. Air Trainer . . . $89.99**
**Punitive Meat Funnel . . . $45.99**
**Treat Pouch . . . $45.99**

**Heavy Petter**

## Poodle Shaver

Shave your poodle down to size with our patented Poodle Shaver.

Scientists have shown that the average poodle is 78 percent fur, but sometimes these super-intelligent dogs can act like they own the place. Teach them a little respect by removing their curly coat.

**DGRDCR. Poodle Shaver . . . $56.87**

*The Poodle Shaver!*

*"A real status flipper—helped me regain the psychological edge over my poodle, Mozart."*
—Pete Marmel, English Teacher

*Before*

*"I'd shave a poodle hard . . ."*
—Dr. Spero Nicholas, Scientist

*What's up, bitch?!*

# Blitzkrieg Your Way Through the Year's Best Couples-Therapy Books . . .

## . . . In less time than it takes to read a fortune cookie!

It's a big problem for every up-and-coming CEO: you're not caught up on your couples-therapy homework, and it just keeps piling up. The theory is that you're a dude, and she's working on it and you're not. Now you can beat her at her own game.

### "OFF MY BACK" RELATIONSHIP-BOOK SUMMARIES

While you are off philandering, our smart young assistants are watching out for all the year's new relationship books. We throw out the dead wood: stuff about communicating, anything having to do with birth canals or yoga. We keep the cream of the crop, the 1.9 percent of relationship books that will make you look totally caught up.

Then what? Well, we create a one-sentence written summary and a ten-second audio summary of each book. Some examples:

• *Men are from Mars, Women Are from Venus*: Guys and gals are kind of on different planets, so go to your cave.

• *Getting the Love You Want*: Start every fight with "What I hear you saying is . . ."

• *The Seven Principles of Marriage*: Fondness, Sharing, Bargaining, Denial, Grouchy, Sneezy, and Doc.

Done. Boom. Time to get loaded.

# "Off My Back" Relationship– Book Summaries®

## 2.5 MINUTES IS ALL IT TAKES

Scientists say that you actually learn more from hearing just someone's good ideas than from hearing *all* their ideas.

Think of all the therapy books you have been told to read by your spouse or therapist, or even required to read as a part of a court-ordered anger-management program. With our lightning-quick summaries, you could have saved literally millions of hours!

## A PERSONAL THERAPY BOOK READER TO HELP YOU CATCH UP

We will be your personal therapy-book reader, so you don't have to do it yourself.

Every three weeks, you will be sent summaries of best-selling therapy books like:

- *Loving Too Hard*
- *Oops, You Ignored My Dreams*
- *Healing Touch of the Bonobo Monkey*
- *Making Lemonade out of Adultery and Hookers*
- *Marriage Plumbing*
- *Chicken Soup for the Multi-Orgasmic Couple*
- *Getting to "Fuck You!"*
- *Marriage Secrets of the Waffen SS*

... and so so so many more!

## PICK YOUR POISON: A FORMAT THAT BEST SUITS YOUR LIFESTYLE

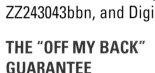

Our summaries come in written and voice-recorded formats, and are also available in "information superhighway" formats such as .ZIP, Linus-MX Powersort, PhotoDangler, ZZ243043bbn, and DigiDonkey.

## THE "OFF MY BACK" GUARANTEE

If this is not working out for you, call us and we will actively listen to what you are saying, and also what's behind what you are saying. We will validate your feelings and try to let our good feelings about you outweigh the negative ones.

*You'll save literally millions of hours!*

# CALL NOW TO ORDER!

Call toll free any time of day or night. Our operators are wearing nothing but cotton panties, but they are real tomboys, so don't let them talk your ear off about the playoffs. Naughty college tramps!

**RLTBKS. Written service . . . $99.00/mo.**
**Recorded Service . . . $89.99**
**Sorry, not interested . . . $109.99**

## *Get "Off My Back" Now!*

# gnomes & **gardens**

## Executive Bullfrog Pump

How do you think they get like that? Magic? Stop complaining about the world and start doing something about it! Will pump up a toad in nine seconds.

**FROGPMPR. Bullfrog Pump . . . $99.00**

## gnomes & **gardens**

*Impress your neighbors!*

*Take it to the limit—the legal limit!*

## You Don't Need to Be a Lawyer to Install this Slammin' Law Library in Your Own Home

Surprise your house guests when you're out back having a Rob Roy and a smoke. If someone says something, you can answer with, "Hmm. I wonder if there's any precedent for that?" . . . and then lead them into your cherried-out legal-research pod!

**SCMARTST. Law Library . . . $1,999.00**

*Some of the books are fake, with ample hiding space behind them for your top-secret legal assistant: booze!*

# gnomes & **gardens**

## Young Grandma Yardwork Set

You had Jennie when you were 17; don't pretend you were shocked when Jennie had Terry and Cody when she was the same age—now you've got some babysittin' duties, Grandma!

This rake and jack-o'-lantern leaf bag will help you keep the kids busy while Jennie and her date hook up on the couch and then sleep off their hangovers.

**DMSLYU. Young Grandma Yardwork Set . . . $25.99**

## *Bridges of Madison County* Commemorative Mailbox

Cry, cry, cry . . . cry me a river. This lonesome dove of a sad sleepy snowy mailbox will be perfect for sending and receiving drippy love letters.

**SDMLBX. Madison Mailbox . . . $88.99**

## Apology Snapper

The ancient Romans coined the words "mea culpa," meaning, literally, "take these fish." Rubber fisherman's gloves and a satchel of snapper will make the act of contrition easy.

Say it with seafood.

**SRYFSH. Apology Snapper . . . $19.99**

## gnomes & gardens

### Vegetarian-Be-Gone Totem

Ward off vegetarians with this HUGE donkey head or elk head or whatever it is. Lovingly stuffed with donkey-stuffing. Scare the hippies right out of any dinner party.

**VEGHED. Vegan Scarer . . . $99.99**

### Orange Rock with Jesus' Face

Each of our authentic orange rocks has a miracle image of the Saviour's face. Just keep looking, you'll see it.

**JESSRK. Rock of Ages Holy Orange Stone . . . $10.00**

### Petrified Frozen Yogurt

Did the cavemen have soft serve? Looks like it!

This replica of petrified frozen yogurt was probably made by the Thessol-Honkeys in 459 B.F.

Now you can be a historical part of owning one of these things.

**RCKCNDY. Ancient Dessert Sculpture . . . $999.66**

# gnomes & **gardens**

**"Wow."**
—Tony Shen, CEO

*"Die Noodlebristle"*

*"Bambeza"*

*"El Swep"*

*"帚"*

## "Brooms of the World" Collectors Set

From the Portuguese *vassoura* to the German *Besen*, the broom has been a staple of sweeping and the go-to guy of the domestic-chore sphere since the early hominids first swept their dingo huts. Imported exclusively for gnomes & gardens, this throat-tighteningly bashed-up set of genuine brooms comes from the four corners of the world. The bristles are hand-selected by our janitorial panel and then rigorously tested by a team of sweepers.

Join our Broom of the Month Club, and receive a new broom each month for 1,200 months: that's 100 years of brooms!

**BR29843. Broom Club . . . $56.99 per broom**

ORDER NOW
AND RECEIVE A
FREE CROATIAN
FERTILITY BROOM!

# gnomes & gardens

## Honor Your Loved Ones with a Poetic Garden Bench

This wooden bench is beaten with a motorcycle chain just for the hell of it. Designed by artist Noam Bryzinski, each bench is engraved with a bilious poem.

**BNCH. Poetic Garden Bench . . . $199.99**

### Choose from Three Verses . . .

#### Step-Grandpa
*It's no secret I hated your guts for a while.*
*I was so protective of Nonni,*
*but you really lit a fire under her ass.*
*I didn't think old people should get married again,*
*but your love proved me wrong.*

#### Cousin
*You are my dad's sister's daughter*
*But I think you are so freaking h-t*
*Do U want 2 get coffee?*

#### Little Uncle
*You are still a baby,*
*But you are my uncle.*
*I guess that's what happens*
*when Grandmas*
*get pregnant.*
*I love you, Little Uncle.*

## This Sarcastic Sun Face Will Keep Shining Through Your Crumbling Marriage

You and Ron weren't really very compatible, and now that the kids have left, things seem especially hollow—but check out this purse-lipped sun-face sculpture! Divert you and your guests' attention from your impending divorce. The verdigris, corrosion-proof plaque has a look that is both wistful and disappointed.

**SUNFAC. Happy/Sad Sun Face . . . $89.99**

# gnomes & **gardens**

## Gopher Stompers

If there's anyone out there who actually likes gophers, please give us a call.

Hello?

Our phone is not ringing, and neither is your lawn.™

Strap these Gopher Stompers on your shoes and stroll around your yard, maybe put Steely Dan on your iPod. It will be quiet and peaceful above, but down below it will look like Vietnam meets Frankenstein.

**GPHRSTMP. Gopher Stompin' Strap-ons . . . $29.99**

## Turn Any Gravestone into a Sailboat!

Your grandpa maybe always wanted to be a sea captain in life—maybe he didn't, but why not let him keep on sailing with a handsome ship's wheel that will turn any headstone into the helm of a schooner.

Fun and respectful.

**GRVBOT. Grave Boat . . . 499.00**

## gnomes & gardens

## Wicker Spaniel Trap

Are you turning a blind eye to a spaniel infestation in your own home or yard? Be they springer, cocker, or Cavalier King Charles, they will be caught by this spring-loaded and super-tight wicker dog catcher.

Bait the trap with some meat or a spaniel bitch, sit back, and let the magic happen.

**2PETA99. Spaniel Trap . . . $50.00**

## Hummingbird Poisoner!

Tired of these little nuisances drinking all your nectar? Our Hummingbird Poisoner will wipe out up to 1,000 hummingbirds per day!

**P2PB. Hummingbird Poisoner . . . $99.00**

**Two PoySun packs + The Doors "Greatest Hits" CD . . . $23.99 ea.**

# You Can Set a World Record for How Happy You Are. Guaranteed.

Who wouldn't like that? Who wouldn't like to set a record for how happy and powerful they are?  The answer is nobody.

Nobody but a complete idiot.

Hi. You know me. I'm Blaine Cardoza. Twelve years ago, I delivered the keynote at a mandatory men's retreat in Sebastopol. I called it "Blaine Cardoza's Three Pillars to Achieving World Record Happiness." I didn't think it was a big deal. I was just trying to share some really simple tips that helped me become a bestselling author, triple-green-belt tiger-style karate instructor, and future racecar driver.

But you know what?  Afterwards, men came up to me and said, "Stop! That was unbelievable!" And the rest, as they say, is history.

Now fast-forward to now. The course that has changed so many lives is now available to you on a multimedia CD-ROM format.  It will introduce you to my personal system, called Blaine Cardoza's Three Pillars to World Record Power and Happiness.

What's a pillar? A pillar is a support—an idea or belief that can change your life. Let me explain what I mean.

A multimedia system from the same self-improvement wizard who brought you *Houston, We Have a Proble-tunity* and *Vice President of My Own Life.*

### PILLAR #1:  IF SUCCESSFUL PEOPLE HAVE ONE THING, IT'S STRENGTH.

The first pillar is Strength. Do I mean moral strength? No. Strength of character? No. I'm talking about punching out a police horse. Throwing a bowling ball through a fish tank. Raw physical strength. You get it by learning the pillars, following the steps on the CD-ROM and smoking a little PCP.  That is the Blaine Cardoza System.

### PILLAR #2:  BEND, DON'T BREAK; STRENGTH IS NOTHING WITHOUT TOLERANCE.

The Second Pillar is Tolerance. It doesn't matter if a person is black or white, gay or straight, **they are going to try to get you.** And when they do, you need tolerance. To pain. Pain tolerance is one of my favorite parts of the Cardoza system. I'll give you an example: a student of mine who had been using

*"They gave me PCP. What do I do? Bend the jail bars, get out, make a star map, catch a deer."*

my system for only six hours literally flew off his balcony . . . onto a tractor. And you know what he said to me? "Thank you."

Here's another example from my own life: I'm no Hobbit, but I do like jewelry . . . so what do I do? Using my system, I pull an engagement ring out of a french fry cooker! I show you the ring on the CD-ROM.

### STOCKHOLM, SWEDEN, 1999: "USING HIS SYSTEM, BLAINE CARDOZA STUNS A WHOLE TOWN"

In an ambulance racing through the city streets of Stockholm, I got some great news: I had set yet another world record! This time it was for kicking through the windshield of a tour bus. I just smiled. I didn't even really need the ambulance, but people wouldn't understand. But you can understand, in a short period of time, using my CD-ROM system.

### PILLAR #3 EAST MEETS WEST: INTEGRATING WHAT THESE GUYS OVER HERE ARE DOING WITH WHAT THOSE GUYS OVER THERE WANT TO DO.

Martial Arts. Buddha. Sudoku. Sushi. All Ancient. All mysterious . . . until you study the third pillar of my system. Press "play" on CD #3 and prepare to have your mind blown.

> Finally, a motivational system based on a results-proven drug: PCP.

### THE AMAZING BACKGROUND STORY

Let me tell you where the system comes from. I studied at/near Stanford University in the '60s and took part in their famous psychology experiment in a locked facility. They gave me PCP. What do I do? I bend the jail bars, get out, make a star map and catch a deer. But the professor who visited me the next day told me, "Blaine, we didn't give you PCP; that was a placebo." That's a sugar pill, folks. You see, I had unleashed the natural power of PCP in my mind. That night, I developed my whole system. I found out later that they had actually given me a lot of PCP. So what. It's there, waiting to be unleashed: prime the pump. You gotta use a little PCP to get a little PCP.

Order now, and start unlocking the three pillars that will catapult you into World Record Happiness.

CD-ROM #1. Strength . . . $149.00
CD-ROM #2. Tolerance . . . $149.00
CD-ROM #3. East Meets West . . . $149.00

**Value Package: Buy the entire system and receive a $50.00 discount plus a bonus gift: *Blaine Cardoza's Pocket Guide To Internet Reverse Porn Stings***

# Mouth Full O'Shitake

fancy foods from around the world

## Our Cutest Little Rat Appetizer

Pop these vermin, rats, and mice into your guests' open mouths and watch them say, "Ooohhhhh." Our appetizing rodent hors d'ouvres are the tasty invention of Head Chef Darryn Steegen from the famous New York eatery "Ollo du Merde." Comes in two flavors, sweet or savory, and three sizes, wharf rat, lab rat, or titmouse. Arrives cryo-packed in hordes of 24.

**RATAPP. Rodent Hor's D'ouvre Horde . . . $49.00**
**(contains actual rat meat)**

## Corn on the Cob Rebuilder!

Our corn on the cob rebuilder is for you! It's the easiest way to rebuild half-eaten corn into a meaty, full-rowed cob. Just jam the wasted cob into the hole, and "shazam," a ripe tube appears!

**CRNRBLDR. Corn Recobber . . . $15.99**

**Yuck!** ➡ **Yum!**

# Mouth Full O'Shitake

fancy foods from around the world

## Sell By ... NEVER! Stamp

Meat and milk will never go bad in YOUR house. Not when you can just stamp a new date on there. Get peace of mind and a bunch of yogurt in your cereal. It's all just propaganda anyway. Best if eaten by February 12, 2012!!!! Fuck the hippies!!!!

**4EVRSTMP. Food Date Stamp ... $99.00**

## Blueberry Muffin of the Month Club

Get a new blueberry muffin every month. If it has blueberries, and it's a muffin, it's coming to your door. You'll be the king of the blueberry muffin community.

**BLBERY. Blueberry Muncher Club ... $14.00/mo.**

# PUZZLE ME TIMBERS
Games & Puzzles to Blast Away the Boredom

## "The Great Potato Famine" Board Game!

Here's a fun time: Potato Famine is the competitive game that the whole family can have a good time with. Steal your uncle's potato! Raid your teenage niece's potato sack. But make sure your shed is secure, or you may have to take a ship to America, join a gang, and call yourself Baboon Connolly. "Anything can happen in a potato famine."™ Comes with a board and seventeen potatoes. (Not racist. Educational.)

**BBNCNL. Potato Famine Game . . . $45.99**

## Other learning games from SkyMaul:

**Transit Strike!! . . . $9.99**　　**Ethnic Border Bonkers!! . . . $56.99**　　**Eco-Terror Jamboree!! . . . $18.99**

THE PUZZLER

". . . NEARLY IMPOSSIBLE." — STEPHEN HAWKING

## The Puzzler

Who says your girlfriend can't be in MENSA? Introduce some brain food into your foreplay with this intimate logic puzzle. It's a bewildering series of locks and hoops that starts at base camp of your pole and extends as far as your imagination will take you!

**PZLR. The Puzzler . . . $119.99**

# PUZZLE ME TIMBERS
### Games & Puzzles to Blast Away the Boredom

## Crack Pipe Chess Set

"I would play chess, but I'm smoking crack right now." Sound familiar? Not anymore.

Our company has solved that dilemma once and for all: every piece of our crack-pipe chess set is a suckable, hittable pipe. The Game of Kings doesn't have to take a backseat to anything again, including sucking base rock cocaine.

**CRKCHES. Crack Pipe Chess Set . . . $17.90**

**"I'm fired up about trying this."**
—G. Weisert, *Drugs & Games Magazine*

## "Jumble" Book!

Everybody loves Jumble. Now, at last, an entire book, scrambled!

**WRDSLD. Jumble Book . . . $45.99**
**JMBLHB. Jumble Book, Hebrew . . . $46.99**

**"Unsolvable!"**
—Paul "The Puzzler" Stasi

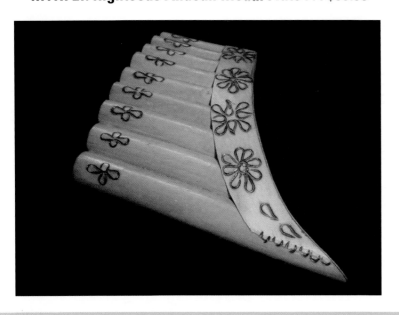

# *The Nicest Gift*

... is to let people deal with stuff on their own.

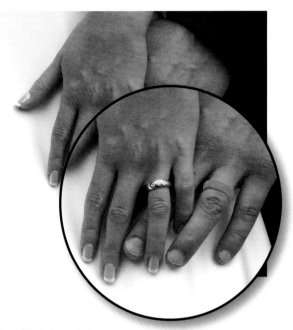

## Men's Skin-Tone Wedding Bands

*You* know you're married. *She* knows you're married. Isn't that enough?™

Wedding rings can be a really . . . you know . . . ugh, it just feels like . . . why? Why do you have to be announcing your marital status to every cocktail waitress that swaggles past? It's just rude.

This product will allow you to wear your wedding ring, but not have to be so in-your-face about it to other people and girls.

**FREDOM. Men's Skin-Tone Band . . . $455.00**
*Whole sizes 6 to 14*

## Sixty-Five-Gallon Wine Glass

Now you can have just one and mean it! Whether you're pregnant or just having a long business lunch, our hot-tub-sized wine glass lets you guzzle bottles of lip-smacking pinot without breaking the letter of the law. "Honeshtly offisher, I only ha-blawwww!"

**BIGWINE. Giant Wine Glass . . . $69.99**

# *The Nicest Gift*

... is to let people deal with stuff on their own.

## "Mom, I fucked up. Can you pick me up?"

### Get-Out-of-Cult Phone Card

A cult is defined as a "young, tacky religion." They're fun and cool for about nine days; then it's time to go back to Berkeley and get high. No shoes? No money? No buffalo wings? No problem. Get out of any cult fast with our convenient, easily concealable phone card.

**HLPMM. $10 Card . . . $13**
**CLTESP. $25 Card . . . $52**

## Junta Backpack and Coup Map

You say you want a revolution? With our stylish leather Junta backpack and coup map, the current regime's days are numbered!

The Junta backpack is roomy and light, sturdy enough for attacking the palace, and stylish enough for going out clubbing.

**LTRJNT. Revolution Backpack . . . $89.99**

## Hamster Ring

Our genuine hamster ring combines one of the cutest animals with one of the most popular pieces of jewelry: the ring!

This furry little wiggly friend is attached with humane "FunStitches" to a pewter band, allowing the whole assembly to slip neatly onto your finger. It's the perfect way to tell your significant other that there's something deeply wrong with you.

**HMSTR. Hamster Ring . . . $99.00**
**Muzzle for hamster . . . $12.00**

# The Nicest Gift
... is to let people deal with stuff on their own.

## Virgin-Mary-Holding-Baby-Spock Stained Glass Window

For the first time ever, the Virgin Mary has been brought together with First Officer Spock as a lad! This touching scene, depicted in perfect detail in stained glass, shows Mary holding the miniature leader of the USS *Enterprise*'s whole science department while he puzzles over Klingon words. Ridiculous.

**MNASPCK. Mary and Spock . . . $999.99**

## Argument-Starter Ornament

This beautiful bulb shows an unborn little guy just snoozing his way through Grinch-mas time. Quietly drape your tannenbaum with a bakers dozen of these fully formed human angels, and when Kurt and Lisa visit from San Fran-gay-sco, your tree will ignite a holiday argue-sation!

**FTSBLB. Argument Ornament . . . $19.99/dozen**

# Banana Hammockslammer

## Print Your Own Money!

Who says you can't print your own money?

This industrial strength printing press has been used by some of the most famous governments, but will still fit conveniently into your blue Dodge van.

Nothing beats the satisfaction of spending money that you made yourself.

**MIDAS2K. Money Maker . . . $4,999.99**

## Adultery Detector

Has your husband been cheating on you with the dental hygienist, the librarian—maybe even your best friend? What about with some stewardesses? An IM chat buddy? The cops? The Navy? The Jehovah's Witnesses?

Find out. Now.

Our steam-powered adultery detector has a nozzle that blows detective-strength steam into a jacket, pants or shirt and then sucks the evidence back into a CheaterSak. Give the convenient Sak to your attorney, and bingo: Alimony!

**BRKBCK. Cheater Detector . . . $49.99**

# Banana Hammockslammer

# 2-DADZ
## Role-playing Kit

More and more men are having babies. Wherever you live and however you think, you need to be prepared to understand how a dual-father household works. This pregnancy simulator will help you get in the mind-set of the new millennium— the "2 Dadz" millennium!

**DADZPGNT.
Mr. and Mr. Mom . . . $59.99**

# Banana Hammockslammer

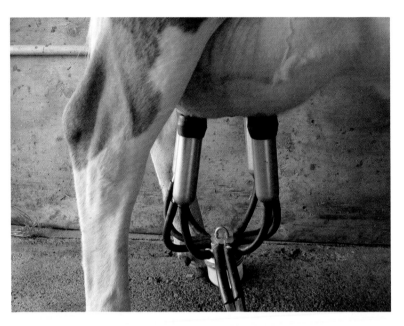

## Cow Charger

It's cold, and your cow won't get up. What's wrong with her? We don't know, but it sounds like an electrical problem. These cow jumper cables will get a cow started with a gentle jolt that feels to a cow much like what a cup of coffee might feel like to an infant—a new, fun, what-do-I-do-with-myself kind of vibe.

**CWCHRG. Cow Charger . . . $179.99**

## HUMMER 6: Post-Rapture Edition

No gas left. Oil fields burning. Not many of us left here at the factory . . . Zombie "people" trying to get in. Water running low.

**ENDWLD. Hummer 6 . . . Will trade for child-bearing woman or coal or meat.**

Zombie H6 Escaper — Limited Edition

# Banana Hammockslammer

## This "Smart" Clock Will Make Your Brain Explode

This um-mazing time machine has three elliptical orbits: the moon, the earth, and . . . no. Start over: it has TWO orbits, but three elliptical centers, such that each ellipsis intersects its opposite's orbit at precisely the hour of the greatest distance from . . . Wait. That doesn't work. The longest circumference synchronizes with—You know what? Fuck it. You figure it out, genius.

**CRZYCLK. Mind Bender Time Device . . . $299.88
Comes with martini shaker and *Golf's
Greatest Hole in Twos* DVD.**

## Gay Wormhole Between Two Dimensions

Travel from Fire Island to Berlin 1932 in no time through this gay wormhole between parallel dimensions.

**GAYSLNKY.
Gay Time Travel . . . $1,999.88**

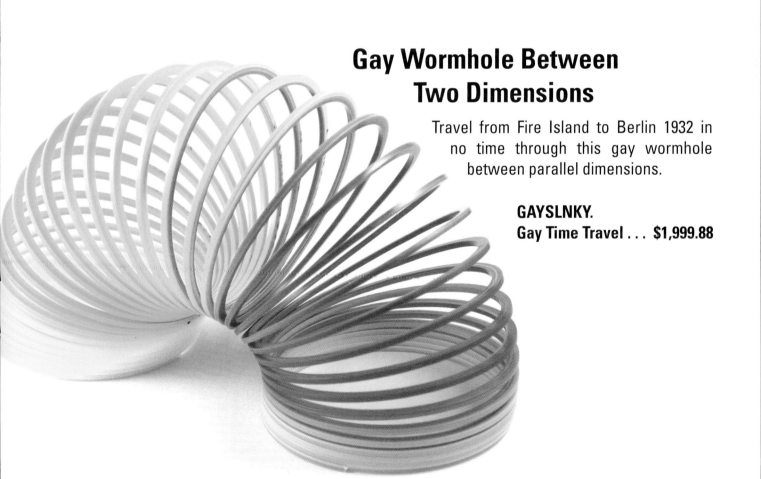

# *Back Door Slider*

Sneaking sports into your house the old-fashioned way . . . by mail

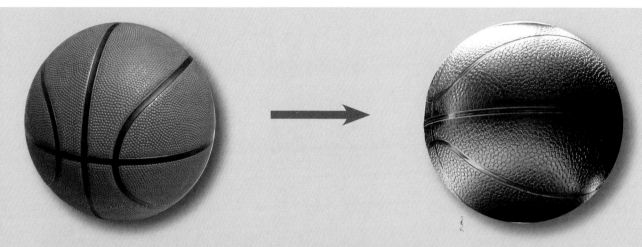

## Turn Your Basketball into Solid Gold

Have you ever heard anyone say, "I'd like to buy an ounce of basketball"? No. *There's a reason for that.*

Now you can turn your basketball into valuable solid gold. You and your college friends can have the financial freedom needed to live on a farm together and write music and comedy, or have a band or a company together. Using our converter, turn an honest basketball into a lip-smearing chunk of valuable GOLD!

**MDSBAL. Gold Basketball Maker . . . Call for price.**

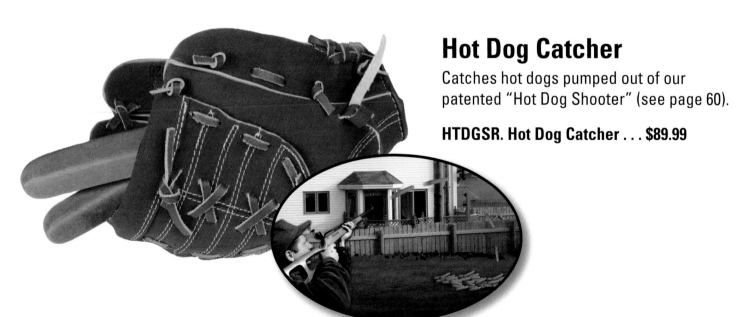

## Hot Dog Catcher

Catches hot dogs pumped out of our patented "Hot Dog Shooter" (see page 60).

**HTDGSR. Hot Dog Catcher . . . $89.99**

## Back Door Slider

Sneaking sports into your house the old-fashioned way . . . by mail

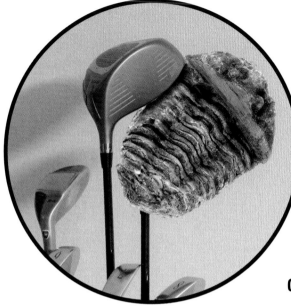

### The Trilobyte Golf Club Cover

Slip this sweet arthropod on your three wood. Sooner or later, your golf partner Alan is bound to say, "What is that dried up piece of crap?" That's your cue to take him to school . . . the school of Trilobita! Throw down your knowledge of these ancient "butterflies of the sea"—Phacops, Metacanthina, Koneprusia, etc.—and mark out the territory of your hobby kingdom. Any questions?

**GLFCVR. Trilobyte Golf Club Covers . . . $78.99**

## Own a Piece of Horse Racing History with Our Commemorative Seabiscuit Statue

This one-of-a-kind Seabiscuit statuette is machined from solid brown material and signed by John Elway. Put it on your mantle, or in the guest room, or who cares? The world's greatest race horse, captured in his retirement, forever draped in a victory robe and showing the Seabiscuit "Hump" that made him so famous.

**SPRTZNT. Chocolate Racehorse . . . $89.99**

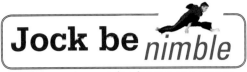

# Jock be *nimble*
### Sports equipment for former superstars

## Skindiving Wristwatch

Our incredible skindiving watch (not shown) tells time and blah blah blah. YESSSSSS!

**SKNWDR. Wristwatch . . . $59.99**

## Tweaker Bike

"It would be cool to have a car, but for now I can get across town and break a sweat on this li'l crankster-gangster's dream." Order this with our Tweaker Cross (p. 46).

**TWKBK. Speed Bike . . . $77.49**

## Police "Partner Yoga" Video

Let the tension evaporate after a hard day on the force, or maybe you want to do some policeman-on-policeman role-playing. Whatever the case, lengthen your limbs and open your mind as you assume the "downward cop" pose. Retired NYPD Captain Darryn Steegan will lead you through eighteen and a half invigorating "asanas."

This kit includes some cop suits and a box of incense.

**PLCYGA. Cop Yoga Instructional Video . . . $99.44**

*"Right to Remain Silent" Pose*

**90 Minutes** of Two Cops Doing Yoga!

*"The Swan"*

Relaxing!

*"The Car Cobra"*

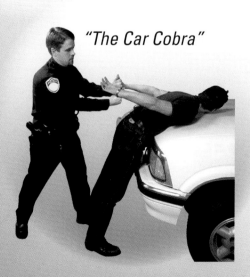

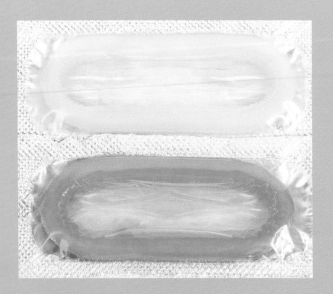

# Mistresses

"Mrs. Calhoun"

"Fat Nan"

"Behind every great man is a great woman, and behind her is another, not-as-great woman to whom he puts the wood."
—Betsy Ross

"Lazy-Eye Lucy"

"Alice Glass"

"The Bungler"

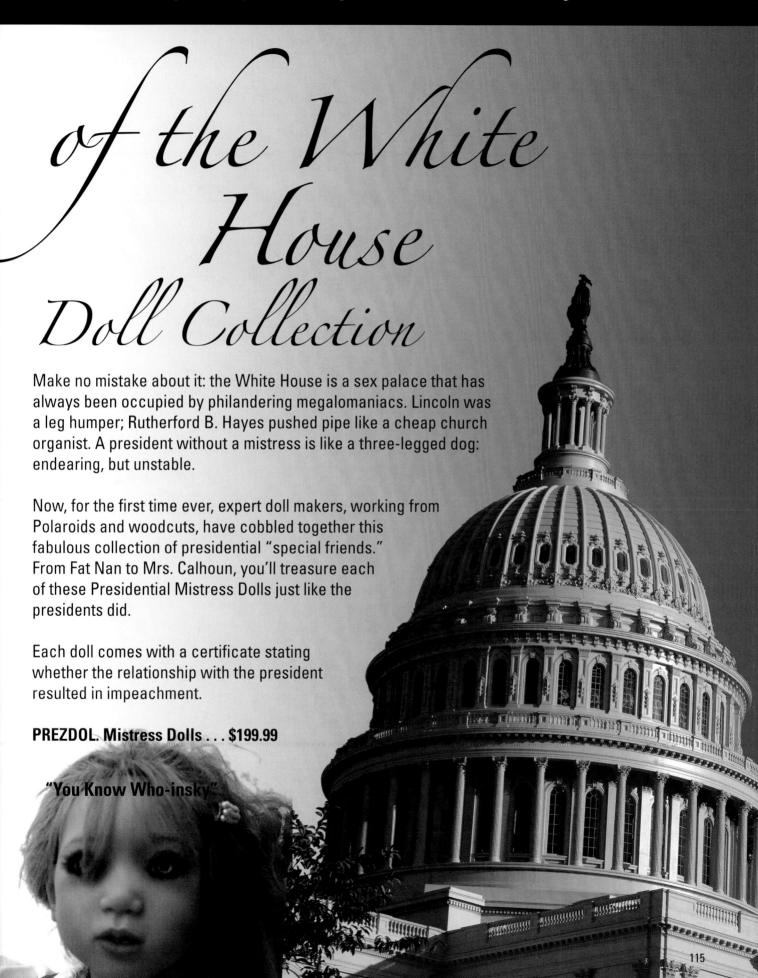

# of the White House
## Doll Collection

Make no mistake about it: the White House is a sex palace that has always been occupied by philandering megalomaniacs. Lincoln was a leg humper; Rutherford B. Hayes pushed pipe like a cheap church organist. A president without a mistress is like a three-legged dog: endearing, but unstable.

Now, for the first time ever, expert doll makers, working from Polaroids and woodcuts, have cobbled together this fabulous collection of presidential "special friends." From Fat Nan to Mrs. Calhoun, you'll treasure each of these Presidential Mistress Dolls just like the presidents did.

Each doll comes with a certificate stating whether the relationship with the president resulted in impeachment.

**PREZDOL. Mistress Dolls . . . $199.99**

"You Know Who-insky"

# Relax and Enjoy Your Trip
## A Free Crossword Puzzle from SkyMaul

# Happy crap you can buy from a plane!

## Across

3. Inca ATV
7. Superman's weakness
9. Mini-hooks on a cat's hands
11. Devours plane crash survivors
12. Hit hard by a big person
14. A very high boy scout
15. A suspicious vehicle that should not be knocked if it is rocking at that time
18. A place with no air or land, much less clouds or trees, but it is not outer space
19. Invented the parachute
20. There is no _____
22. A rough flight
24. Expensive habit
26. Heaviest kind of dwarf
29. Chances of making it to your next birthday "in the event of a water landing"
31. Horse that can poke anything's eye out
34. Brothers and sisters I have none, but this man's father is my father's son; who am I?
35. Jimi Hendrix (to a Hobbit)
37. Whatever that gets timed by itself equals what this is of the thing
39. Place you go when you're depressed
40. A winged horse
41. Godzilla's nemesis

## Down

1. Space scientists that can paralyze someone by giving them a tiny shoulder massage
2. Something one cowboy might say to another
4. Female dog
5. Official drink of the Russian space program
6. Best kind of jumping bean
8. Indian party cactus
10. A brilliant, jobless idealist
13. A recipe combining hamburger, ketchup, and white bread
16. Land where Jesus morphs into a vegan Lion
17. Deadliest type of plane
18. James Dean's resting place
21. You can make your own _____
23. A natural substance used by tree-huggers as deodorant
25. Great honor
27. Cross between a mule and another mule
28. The devil wants us all to do this constantly
30. A heart-stopping thrill ride that rhymes with "dolphin"
32. I said I wanted all my _____, not some of my _____
33. A tiny four-legged Nazi
36. A place where honkies go
38. There is no "I" in "team," but there is _____

# Here They Are: Your Complimentary SkyMaul Crossword Puzzle Answers

# "Now is not a good time . . ."

**Our stockroom is full of products!**

You'll almost never hear these words from a trained SkyMaul operator. We are standing by 24/7 to take your order in a friendly and professional manner. Rarely, you may catch one of us having a moment. We all have our ups and downs, but we're a big family here at SkyMaul. One thing about families is they fight sometimes. Like right now, this operator is not speaking to our C.E.O., Jerry, because he went into the work refrigerator and ate her cottage cheese, even though it was on the shelf that was NOT FOR GENERAL CONSUMPTION. The guy makes two million a year! He could buy a whole cottage fucking cheese *factory.*

Anyway. It's not always us. If you are getting angry at one of our operators, maybe you should look in the mirror. We will try to be nice and answer any questions you have, but if we seem rude to you, could it be, like, partially your fault? Maybe *you're* the butthole/bitch/cocksucker?

You're pissed at us; we're pissed at you. OK. Why don't you and I get in a time machine and travel back to before you started flippng out? Maybe call back, or we'll call you back. Or how about this: you get free shipping. How's that? Do you feel like you "won"? Whatever.

—Customer Relations

# Order Form / Customer Survey

(Please fill In, then fold up and throw out.)

SkyMaul is interested in your shopping experience. Was it good, bad, interesting, very interesting, "trippy"? We are constantly trying to improve our service by learning more about you. Please take a moment to complete our survey. We plug this information into a computer "number blender" and out comes the address labels, preprinted. Unbelievable.

What do you want? _____

Name _____

Address _____

Telephone number (circle) 0 1 2 3 4 5 6 7 8 9 0

Soc. Security Number _____

Birthdate _____

Place of birth (circle one): Bed, Hot Tub, Floor, Dolphin Pool

Height _____

Height on Match.com _____

Ideal Weight _____

Eye color _____

Does the carpet match the drapes? (circle one) Y N

Handedness: (circle one) Right Left Ambi.

Bank acct. number(s) _____

PIN numbers _____

Do you prefer (circle one) riding/pushing lawnmower/doing nothing?

What was your most forgettable sexual experience? _____
_____

What was it like growing up (circle all that apply) poor/rich/bi/mixed? _____
_____

What Christianity are you? (circle one) Jew, Catholic, Muslim, Christian, Double Christian, Cult/Mormon, Burning Man, Pagan/Goddess/Vegan

Do you agree that the world is going to end soon? What? Why not? _____
_____

Privacy policy: SkyMaul holds your private information in the strictest confidence. Your information is shared only with entities who pay SkyMaul anything for it. SkyMaul loves you, and if SkyMaul should ever die, it will come back during the Rapture riding on a donkey and using a laser gun to sort out the good people from the bad.

# Acknowledgments

We would like to thank the following people for their help with this book:

Our agent, Danielle Svetcov, and our editors, Sean Desmond and John Parsley. Liz Craig, Arin Fishkin, Brad Rhodes, Spero Nicholas, Sean Nolan, and Charette Communication Design for generous design support, and Mario Parnell for expert photography. Gabe Weisert, Paul Stasi, Kasey Evans, Trey Marlowe, Ann Torres, Harold Check, Jim Fourniadis, Jacob Goldstein, Dan Mullen, Ross McCall, Spero Nicholas, Don Novello, Dave Owen, Janet Varney, Cole Stratton and SF Sketchfest, MEAT, Marisa Milanese, Mo Lee, Jesse Thorn, and Jeremy Solterbeck for feedback and creative contributions. The fans of Kasper Hauser for years of vital support. The person who actually made the book, Vince Bohner, and Jen and Jack. And most importantly, our families, especially Julie, Laura, Michelle, Ben, and Roberta: thank you for making this book possible.

# About the Authors

KASPER HAUSER is (L to R) Dan Klein, James Reichmuth, John Reichmuth, and Rob Baedeker. The group has headlined many of the best comedy clubs and festivals in the U.S. and won the Herald Angel at the Edinburgh Fringe Festival. They cowrote and starred in the feature films *Fishing with Gandhi* and *Cow Monkey* and have appeared on Comedy Central.

# Photo Credits

Cover photos: adultery, pepper spray, SkyMonkees: Mario Parnell; ring: stock.xchng; llamacyle: iStockphoto.com
Cover design: Vince Bohner

8: CEO: Mario Parnell. 9: headphones, dude: Mario Parnell. 10: shredders: Mario Parnell. 11: bananas: stock.xchng; bandanas: Mario Parnell; whoreganizer: Hemera. 12: dreamcatcher: Mario Parnell; lettuce, dog, turtles, cow, chest: stock.xchng. 13: face melter, toothpaste mask: Mario Parnell. 14: dog, watch, sundial: stock.xchng. 15: blanket: Hemera; llama: iStockphoto.com; wheel: Spero Nicholas; pouch: Hemera; tractor: stock.xchng. 16: toilet, bee, thermometer: Hemera; lantern: Jennifer Marr (stock.xchng) 17: man: Mario Parnell; DVD, puppets: stock.xchng. 18: ear, scale: Hemera. 19: hat: iStockphoto.com; wolf, socket: stock.xchng; baby: Hemera. 20: trumpet, hydrants: stock.xchng. 21: salon namer: stock.xchng; haircut: Julie Elliott (stock.xchng). 22–23: straightener, guys, dog, filter, scientist: Hemera. 24: stroller mower: Hemera; timer: stock.xchng. 25: vacuum, cereal, shuttle: Hemera; bowl: Neil Gould (stock.xchng). 26: robot: stock.xchng; microscope, hands: hemera; beaker, test tubes: stock.xchang. 27: idiot, can: Mario Parnell. 28: red car: stock.xchng; suv: Pete "Langy" Langshaw (stock.xchng); magnet, crotch: KH. 29: toilet, weightlifter: Hemera; coffin: stock.xchng. 30: chair, safe, globes: stock.xchng. 31: gnomes: stock.xchng; guy: Hemera. 32: lion head, figurines: stock.xchng. 33: fist: Hemera; head: stock.xchng. 34: memorial, King Menouch: stock.xchng. 35: friend photo, egg: Hemera; acne poster: stock.xchng. 36–37: chess set: Mario Parnell. 38–40: boats, flowers, lake, road: Gabe Weisert. 41: beach: stock.xchng. 42: sunset, ocean: Gabe Weisert. 43: fire: stock.xchng. 44: 10 Commandments: Deni Montgomery, dreamstime.com; spigot, reverend: Mario Parnell; bible: stock.xchng; couple: Hemera. 45: massage scene: Mario Parnell. 46: cross, beads: stock.xchng. 47: whale: stock.xchng. 48: guy: Mario Parnell; castle, dice, disk: stock.xchng; black laptop, mug, map, donkey: Hemera. 49: pestles: Hemera; picnic, fingernails, pills: stock.xchng. 50: poison: Hemera; plant: stock.xchng. 51: people: Hemera; cookies: stock.xchng. 52: box, decoder ring: stock.xchng. 53: hat: Mario Parnell; welder: Hemera; baggie: stock.xchng; iron panel, window: stock.xchng. 54: map, pillow: Mario Parnell. 55: bike, trinket, pitcher: stock.xchng. 56: soldier: Mario Parnell; medal, flag: stock.xchng; quarters: Hemera. 57: coins, hand, sink: stock.xchng; cannon: Hemera. 58: guy: Hemera; beluga: stock.xchng; globe: Mario Parnell; toast: Hemera. 59: chair: stock.xchng; stool, CD racks: Hemera. 60: mini car: stock.xchng; guy, hot dogs: Hemera; house: stock.xchng. 61: car sled, sea biscuit: stock.xchng. 62–63: guy, crutch: Mario Parnell; watch, necklace, squirrel: stock.xchng. 64: terrier, Chihuahua, robots: stock.xchng. 65: bear: stock.xchng; kitty: Mario Parnell. 66: building, graffiti, spray can: stock.xchng. 67: fire, gladio-bopper, soaps: stock.xchng. 68: bear, hedgehog: stock.xchng; turtles: Erris van Ginkel (stock.xchng). 69: vegetables: stock.xchng; karate belts: Mario Parnell. 70: trophy, skull, kit: stock.xchng. 71: motorcycle, shoes: stock.xchng; llama legs: iStockphoto.com. 72: monks: Gabe Weisert. 73: glass, clubs, mask: Hemera; flask: stock.xchng, 74: pencil sharpener, phantom: Hemera; sock, dolphin stock.xchng. 75: Jesus figurine: Hemera; safe, beans: stock.xchng. 76: food: Hemera; ledger: stock.xchng. 77: guy at table: Mario Parnell; all small images: Hemera. 78: hut, chairs: stock.xchng; clipboard, ice cream: Hemera. 79: dogs: stock.xchng; spray bottle: Hemera. 80: kid: Mario Parnell; little hornets: Hemera; big hornets: stock.xchng. 81: dog surgery, toolbox: stock.xchng; pliers, syringe, dogs: Hemera. 82: tree tiger, grass tiger, climber: stock.xchng; cone dog: Csuka Andràs (stock.xchng); bag: Hemera. 83: kit: Hemera; dog pictures, meerkat: stock.xchng; white dog: Bethan Hazell (stock.xchng); 84: books: Mario Parnell. 85: briefcase, guy at desk: Hemera. 86: Executive: Mario Parnell; bullfrog: Hemera. 87: House: Hemera; library, bottles, bikini, motorbike: stock.xchng. 88: family yard workers, fish: Hemera; mailbox: stock.xchng. 89: moose, rock: stock.xchng; fossil: Stella Reese (stock.xchng). 90: brooms, hand broom: stock.xchng. 91: bench, sun: stock.xchng. 92: gopher stomper: KH; gravestone: stock.xchng; wheel: Hemera. 93: wicker carrier, dog: Hemera; bird feeder: stock.xchng. 94–95: Blaine Cardoza: Mario Parnell; bus: Hemera. 96: food rat: stock.xchng; corn: KH; rebuilder: Hemera. 97: stamp: stock.xchng; meat, muffins: Hemera. 98: game, potatoes: stock.xchng; puzzler: Brad Rhodes. 99: chess set, book: stock.xchng. 100: pipes, mandolin, guitar, instruments: stock.xchng. 101: hands (Petr Kurecka), wine glass: stock.xchng. 102: phone booth, hamster: stock.xchng; backpack: Hemera. 103: stained glass, ornament, fetal image: stock.xchng.104: printer: stock.xchng; detector: Mario Parnell. 105: 2dadz: Mario Parnell. 106: cow: stock.xchng; bike: Phillip Collier (stock.xchng). 107: clock, slinky: stock.xchng. 108: basketballs: stock.xchng; mitt: Hemera. 109: pitcher, golf clubs, trilobyte: Hemera; camel figurine: stock.xchng. 110: snorkler, bike: stock.xchng. 111: jumping jock, police partners, tape, cuffs: Hemera; candle: stock.xchng. 112: dial, Chaplin doll: stock.xchng; condoms: Hemera. 113: puzzler: Brad Rhodes; banana, meter: stock.xchng. 114–115: flag, dolls: stock.xchng; Capitol: iStockphoto.com 116,118: plane: stock.xchng. 119: CDs: Hemera. 121: operator: Mario Parnell; stockroom: stock.xchng. 123: Kasper Hauser: Lisa Keating.

(KH=Kasper Hauser)